Theresa Hak Kyung Cha (1951–1982)

An Hachette UK Company
www.hachette.co.uk

First published in Great Britain in 2018 by Cassell
Illustrated, a division of
Octopus Publishing Group Ltd
Carmelite House
50 Victoria Embankment
London EC4Y 0DZ
www.octopusbooks.co.uk

Distributed in the US by Hachette Book Group
1290 Avenue of the Americas
4th and 5th Floors, New York, NY 10104

Distributed in Canada by Canadian Manda Group
664 Annette St, Toronto,
Ontario, Canada M6S 2C8

ISBN 978 1 78840 064 0

A CIP catalogue record for this book is available
from the British Library.

Printed and bound in China
10 9 8 7 6 5 4 3 2 1

Commissioning Editor Romilly Morgan
Senior Editor Pauline Bache
Copy Editor Alison Wormleighton
Assistant Editor Ellie Corbett
Art Director and Designer Yasia Williams-Leedham
Illustrators Hélène Baum, Miriam Castillo, Sara
Netherway, Shreyas Krishnan, Lauren Simkin
Berke, Allegra Lockstadt, Winnie T Frick, Grace
Helmer, Tanya Heidrich, Marcela Quiroz, Maria
Hergueta
Senior Production Manager Peter Hunt
Production Controller Katie Jarvis

FORGOTTEN WOMEN

THE WRITERS

ZING
TSJENG

CASSELL
ILLUSTRATED

Contents

INTRODUCTION 6

or most of history, Anonymous was a woman." It's a line attributed to Virginia Woolf but is, interestingly, not exactly what she said. The closest she comes to it is in *A Room of One's Own* – an extended essay that is in itself about women writing fiction – with the words, "Indeed, I would venture to guess that Anon, who wrote so many poems without signing them, was often a woman."[1] It's not known who adapted Woolf's prose into that pithy one-liner, but in the spirit of both the original and the altered quote, it would be nice to think that it was a woman.

For this third book in the *Forgotten Women* series, I wanted to pick a subject close to my own heart. I knew the exact point at which I started wanting to become a writer. When I was six, I came across a short story that my elder brother had written in class, and I was completely thunderstruck by a phrase he coined to describe someone shouting. He said that they were "screaming blue bloody murder".

What did it mean? It made me think of an avalanche screeching off the top of a snow-capped mountain, of ice and earth coming together in a violent roar. (We had gone on a family holiday to the Blue Mountains in Australia, which is probably how I made the connection between a natural landscape and the colour blue.)

With the benefit of hindsight and an expensive arts degree, I know that my brother probably mixed up the expression "screaming bloody murder" with its lesser-used cousin, "screaming blue murder". But his imperfect phrasing has always stuck with me as my first encounter with the sheer visual power of language. An elegant turn of phrase can feel utterly right without being part of the accepted vernacular. When a linguistic slip-up dislodges something totally new in your mind, that's the power of good writing.

You don't have to use fancy lab equipment or invest in oil paints to be a writer. Unlike science or art, literature is one of the few disciplines with relatively low overheads. Technically speaking, all you need is a literary voice and something with which to record it. But as any aspiring author will tell you, there is a vast gulf between writing something down and getting it published – and for most of history, it was women's manuscripts that languished at the bottom of the reject pile.

Every year, the US-based non-profit organization VIDA: Women in Literary Arts releases the VIDA Count – a survey of 39 major literary publications and journals that tallies the gender of the authors and critics represented on their pages. The most recent results make for grim reading. Women make up only a third of those in print, and further data suggests that women from ethnic minorities make up a depressingly tiny segment of published authors.[2]

The passage of time does not guarantee progress, either. A study of 104,000 novels written over the last 200 years revealed that there were actually more women authors in Victorian times than in the first half of the 20th century, with a dramatic effect on female representation in fiction itself. The researchers, who were from the University of California at Berkeley and the University of Illinois, wrote:

Women invent female characters much more often than men do, so any decline in the number of women writers will create a corresponding decline in description of women. And there was, in fact, a fairly stunning decline in the proportion of fiction writers who were women, from the middle of the nineteenth century to the middle of the twentieth.

Women go from representing almost half the authors of fiction, to barely a quarter. If this trend is real, it is an important fact about literary history that ought to be foregrounded even, say, in anthology introductions.[3]

In 2015, the novelist Kamila Shamsie issued a passionate call in the *Guardian* newspaper for publishers to devote a single year to publishing female authors, and only female authors, to fix gender inequality in the industry. She optimistically gave them until 2018, reasoning that the experiment would work best in the centenary year of women over 30 receiving the right to vote in the UK. In 2018, just one publisher heeded her call. Shamsie's self-described "provocation"[4] remained just that – a provocation.

Yet there is nothing provocative about giving women writers and their stories equal billing with men. It makes intuitive sense, not least because women read more than men and account for over half of the book-buying public. I prefer, however, to think of it as a matter of historical accuracy.

Long before Woolf called for a room of one's own, women were putting pen (reed, quill or the equivalent medieval writing tool) to paper (or parchment, vellum, clay). They composed epic verse, sly morality tales, philosophical treatises, semi-biographical verse and dystopian science fiction. They were inspired by everything from queer romance to primordial goddess worship, colonial independence struggles, class anxiety, space technology, endangered wildlife and Jesus.

Some toiled in abject poverty; others enjoyed a life of wealth and luxury. A few achieved worldwide fame in their day, only to fade into obscurity, while many received no recognition at all, posthumously or not. There are even those whose works were almost completely lost to time. But all of them saw something within themselves that was worth putting down in print. These are some of the lives contained in *Forgotten Women: The Writers*.

Women's writing is often wrongly maligned as being one-note – the kind of restricted view that sees "women's fiction" receive its own aisle in bookshops when men are allowed to sprawl, unbidden, across every genre and time period. If there is anything that this book shows, it is that women have been writing on all topics of all kinds since time immemorial.

Selecting the women for this book was incredibly tricky, as it has been for all the books in the series. I was fortunate to be assisted in this regard by my editors, Romilly Morgan, Pauline Bache and Ellie Corbett, as well as Dr Gina Luria Walker of The New Historia initiative at The New School. We wanted to represent a wide variety of voices in as many literary disciplines as possible. Though there were dozens more that I wish we could have included, I hope we have at least modestly succeeded in this aim. As Gina put it in one email, "The women are like a sampling of new species of jewels, mined far away, never set together in this way before."

My wish is that you see *The Writers* as a mere introduction to their stories, and that you use this as a cue to stack your shelves with their books, as well as books by other women. As professionally daunting as it has been to write a book about writers, I hope there is something in here that inspires *you* to write, too. Maybe it's a particularly good rhyme or a novelist's interesting turn of phrase – your version of my "blue bloody murder".

People say that a way with words is the key to being an author. I'd argue that it is self-belief; before you even commit words to paper, you have to *believe* that you have something worth saying. The women in this book have that in spades, and I hope their confidence rubs off on you, whether or not you consider yourself a writer.

Above all, *The Writers* is a toast to novelists, poets, essayists, editors and reporters alike; from those who wrote poetry at the dawn of the written language (Enheduanna – *see* page 18) to those who pounded out copy in war zones (Marguerite Higgins – *see* page 198).

May their inkwells – and yours – never run dry.

Poets &
Playwrights

SAPPHO

You've probably heard of Sappho (*c.*620–*c.*570 BC). She gifted the term "sapphic" to the world, and her island birthplace Lesbos is the origin of the word "lesbian". She is probably the most studied poet in this book by a long shot. But what do we actually know about her? Not a lot, as it turns out.

Sappho is thought to have written nine books of lyric poetry so sublime that Solon, an esteemed Athenian lawmaker, desired to learn one by heart "because once I've learned it, I can die".[1] The term "lyric" also references the lyre that was intended to accompany her heart-rending exaltations of love and longing. Sappho's work was meant to be sung, and she is even thought to have invented a plectrum for plucking the strings of the lyre.

Sometime around the Middle Ages, however, almost all of Sappho's work was lost. Only about 260 fragments have been discovered – some consisting of just a few stanzas, and others a few words, mostly copied on shreds of papyrus and parchment. Some were even found buried in an ancient garbage dump in Egypt. So far, only a single complete poem has been found, written in what is now known as sapphic stanza. It's a hymn to Aphrodite, the goddess of love, in which Sappho beseeches her to lend her assistance in a love affair: "Come to me now – release me from these troubles, everything my heart longs to have fulfilled, fulfill, and you be my ally."[2]

The *Suda*, a 10th-century Byzantine encyclopedia of Greek and Roman antiquity, says that Sappho flourished sometime between 612 BC and 608 BC, though the information it provides may not be wholly accurate. (It also describes her marriage to a trader called Kerkylas of Andros – a name that basically translates as "Little Prick from the Isle of Man".) What we do know is that Sappho was enormously fêted in her own time; Plato called her The Tenth Muse – the nine preceding Sappho, of course, were divine mythological beings, the daughters of gods. She was named The Poetess by her contemporaries (Homer, for the record, was called The Poet).

Though now her name is synonymous with queer desire, women from the island of Lesbos, including Sappho herself, were widely associated during her time with heterosexual promiscuity. (In classical Greek, the word *lesbiazein* actually refers to giving fellatio.) Still, various texts – the *Suda* among them – maintain that Sappho was well known for her "shameful friendship"[3] with women. One biographical note, written a few centuries after her death, sniffs: "She has been accused by some of being irregular in her ways and a woman-lover."[4]

In Sappho's time, poetry was mainly performed for ceremonial or religious purposes. Though scholars now question just how autobiographical some of her work is, Sappho dragged the literary form into the realm of the intensely personal and the erotic. "I would rather see her lovely step," Sappho writes of a beautiful maiden named Anaktoria, "and the radiant sparkle of her face than all the war chariots in Lydia and soldiers battling in arms."[5] She was also adept at portraying the queasy physicality of desire:

Once again Love, that loosener of limbs,

bittersweet and inescapable, crawling thing,

seizes me.[6]

As the centuries passed, squeamish historians found ways to explain away Sappho's apparent love of women. In the 19th century, the fad was to pass her off as the head of a girls' school; her adoration of pupils was therefore chaste and purely academic. Another explanation held that she was a priestess to a goddess, and hence her interest in women was purely divine. (Of course, none of these theories accounts for the fact that Sappho could be a teacher or a religious practitioner *and* fancy women at the same time.) Others simply sought to eradicate the question from the face of the earth, like Pope Gregory VII, who some believe ordered the burning of Sappho's manuscripts.

In 2014, a new fragment of papyrus, now called "The Brothers Poem", came to light. Ten years earlier, three fragments had been discovered, making up an almost complete poem known as "The Tithonus Poem". Still, so much has been lost – these are mere shreds of Sappho's entire body of work, and everything else must lie in wait of discovery. No wonder classicists often direct people to the entry on Sappho in Monique Wittig and Sande Zeig's book *Lesbian Peoples: Material for a Dictionary* – a single blank page. Like the objects of her affection, Sappho remains tantalizingly out of reach.

ENHEDUANNA

f you ever visit visit the Mesopotamia storage vault of Penn Museum in Philadelphia, you might encounter a ceremonial stone disc about the size of a large wheel of cheese. It bears a dedication on its back to the Sumerian moon god Nanna from the high priestess of the ancient city of Ur. The front of the carving bears her likeness, with a figure in tiered robes and ornate braids. Meet Enheduanna (*c.*2285–*c.*2250 BC), the woman who is history's first-ever identifiable author.

Enheduanna composed a total of around 42 works, and archaeologists have found records that point to evidence that her poetry survived for centuries – clay tablets of her work were still being created 500 years after her time, suggesting that she was remembered long after her death. Her hymns are the first record of a new and distinct method of worship – one with a personal, revelatory and even sensual relationship with the divine – and her fingerprints can be seen farther along the centuries in the Homeric Hymns of Ancient Greece and the Hebrew Bible.

Enheduanna was already using reeds to carve her words into wet clay tablets only about three hundred years after cuneiform script was even invented. When the Akkadian Empire (*see* page 20) crumbled, these objects vanished in the deserts of present-day southern Iraq until their excavation in the early part of the 20th century. And what glorious poetry they revealed, with lines that transformed sex into jaw-droppingly explicit ritual worship:

My vulva field is open

this maid asks who will plow it.

Vulva moist in the floodlands

the queen asks who brings the ox[7]

Enheduanna was the daughter of Sargon the Great, the powerful king who conquered much of Mesopotamia to establish the world's first empire, the Akkadian Empire. His domain stretched from the fertile Tigris–Euphrates Valley all the way into Turkey. The royal princess was appointed by her father as high priestess and acted as the earthly embodiment of Ningal, the reed goddess who was Nanna's consort. Epic hymns with lines like "peg my vulva / my star-sketched horn of the Dipper / moor my slender boat of heaven / my new moon crescent beauty"[8] were performed by priestesses like Enheduanna as part of rituals that promised fertility and new life to the kingdom.

Her practical function, however, was to unite all the disparate and quarrelsome cities under the banner of religion – a job that involved ruling over an administration of temple officials, overseeing the temple estate and performing all the complex daily rituals that guaranteed the kingdom prosperity and good harvest. Enheduanna must have excelled in all three – over the next half a millennium, Sargon's descendants made sure that princesses like Enheduanna continued to occupy the important position.

Enheduanna's ecstatic hymns celebrated her gods, but above all her divine patron Inanna. Her best-known work is a cycle of three epic poems that hail this fierce warrior goddess, an avatar of fertility and love who is now seen as the early precursor to Ishtar and Aphrodite. The goddess has many faces, and Enheduanna praises her above all else. In one of the epic poems, Enheduanna the devotee salutes Inanna's brute strength:

Lady of blazing dominion

clad in dread

riding on fire-red power

Inanna

holding a pure lance

terror folds in her robes

flood-storm-hurricane adorned

she bolts out in battle

plants a standing shield on the ground.[9]

In another, she coos of the goddess's nurturing side and her king-making power:

To build a house, to build a woman's

chamber, to have implements,

to kiss the lips of a small child are yours,

Inanna,

To give the crown, the chair and the sceptre

of kingship is yours, Inanna. [10]

In her third and final poem in the cycle *The Exaltation of Inanna*, Enheduanna commits some of her own autobiography to verse. She writes of how a man named Lugalanne stages a coup and forces her out of her own temple; left to wander alone in the wilderness, she calls out to Inanna's vengefulness to drive out the usurper, "that you crush rebellious lands...that you smash heads...that you gorge on corpses like a dog".[11] Inanna must have heard her prayers, for the poem ends, happily, with Enheduanna's restoration to priestess.

Enheduanna identified herself throughout her work, staking her historic claim to being the first recorded author of all civilization. Where there were only anonymous scribes before, Enheduanna stepped in to leave her mark on her empire. Her millennia-old voice is still capable of electrifying effect today: "I am Enheduanna, the en-Priestess of Nanna," she writes, addressing her patron goddess. "My lady, I will proclaim your greatness in all the lands and your glory! Your way and great deeds I will always praise!"[12]

AEMILIA LANYER

n 1978, an English scholar made a daring announcement: he'd figured out the identity of William Shakespeare's Dark Lady, the raven-eyed beauty praised in his sonnets. Aemilia Lanyer (1569–1645), an Englishwoman thought to be of Jewish–Italian descent, was the cruel mistress who had driven the Bard himself to distraction. So far so good – except that there was little direct proof that Aemilia had ever crossed paths with Shakespeare, other than some circumstantial evidence courtesy of the records of Aemilia's physician Simon Forman.

What the claims did achieve, however, was to singlehandedly resurrect Aemilia from obscurity, where she had dwelled for some three centuries prior. A new generation of historians pored over Aemilia's history, searching for proof that she was the woman who had inspired Shakespeare. They were met by a writer who was far more than the object of a male author's affections; a ferociously intelligent and inquisitive literary voice who was one of the first women in Britain to publish a book of poetry and the first to seek to make a living off her pen.

In 1569 Aemilia was born in London into the Bassano family, who were musicians by trade – they had originally left Venice to work in the court of Henry VIII. She was only seven when her father died, but the young Aemilia was fortunate enough to be taken in and educated by Susan Bertie, the Dowager Countess of Kent.

Aemilia was 18 when she embarked upon a torrid five-year affair with Elizabeth I's cousin Henry Carey, who was the Queen's Lord Chamberlain and was 45 years Aemilia's senior. Their relationship came to a crashing halt when Aemilia fell pregnant in 1592, and a marriage was swiftly arranged to Alphonso Lanyer, a court musician and occasional military man.

Little is known about Aemilia's life once she fell from Henry's favour, though she reappears in historical records as a tutor to the young Anne Clifford, the daughter of Margaret, Countess of Cumberland. Her illegitimate child with Henry survived, but Aemilia suffered multiple miscarriages when trying to conceive children with Alphonso. In 1597, her medical woes sent her to Forman, who dutifully took note of her complaints and ailments in his case records and then attempted to seduce her while Alphonso was at sea. (It didn't work.)

In 1611, Aemilia did something truly remarkable: she published *Salve Deus Rex Judaeorum* ("Hail, God, King of Jews"), a book of epic poetry that boldly rewrote the Book of Genesis, mostly from the perspective of Pontius Pilate's wife. In the Bible, the unnamed woman is the subject of a single verse in the New Testament, pleading with her husband not to sentence Jesus to death.

Aemilia seizes this scant source material by the throat and makes it sing – in the book's titular poem, Pilate's wife retells the story of creation and mounts an ambitious defence of Eve, and by extension all women:

Then let us haue our Libertie againe,

And challendge to your selues no Sou'raigntie [Sovereignty];

You came not in the world without our paine,

Make that a barre against your crueltie;

Your fault beeing greater, why should you disdaine

Our beeing your equals, free from tyranny?[13]

It is no exaggeration to say that nothing like this had ever been published before. Elizabeth I may have dabbled in poetry, but non-aristocratic women like Aemilia simply did not pick up the quill, let alone produce a book that was bought and sold at bookshops. The first nine poems in the book also make it clear that Aemilia was serious about turning this into a career. Dedicated to high-ranking women like the Queen and the Countess of Dorset, the poems seek to praise and flatter their subjects to obtain their patronage – the sort of patronage that Henry Carey bestowed on Shakespeare's playing company, the Lord Chamberlain's Men, when he became their patron two years after his split with Aemilia.

Unfortunately, Aemilia did not succeed in her quest for patronage. She was 42 when *Salve Deus Rex Judaeorum* came out, and she never published again. We know that she was widowed in 1613, and briefly attempted to run a London school "for the education of noblemen and gentlemen's children of great worth"[14] in 1617. The historical record peters out after that; she was listed as living near her son in London's Clerkenwell before dying in 1645. We may never find out any more about Aemilia Lanyer – or whether she was, indeed, the Dark Lady of Shakespeare's sonnets – but we know enough to call her England's "first feminist poet".[15]

SOR JUANA INÉS DE LA CRUZ

hen Dominican–American writer Julia Alvarez talked back to her parents as a child, her mother would always admonish her: "Don't you try to be a Sor Juana!"[16] The implication was clear: mouthy girls got what they deserved. And there was nobody mouthier than Sor Juana Inés de la Cruz (1651–1695), the 17th-century Mexican nun and poet.

Sor (Sister) Juana was born in 1651 in San Miguel Nepantla, near Mexico City, in what was then called New Spain. She was the illegitimate child of an illiterate criolla woman (a Mexican of Spanish descent) and a Spanish captain who left Juana at her grandfather's hacienda as soon as she turned eight. Juana, however, had more important things on her mind. "Ever since the first light of reason struck me," she remembered, "my inclination toward letters has been so strong and powerful that neither the reprimands of others – I have had many – nor my own reflections – I have engaged in more than a few – have sufficed to make me abandon this natural impulse that God placed in me."[17]

She was barely three years old when she begged an elder sister's tutor to teach her to read and write, and at six or seven was already imploring her mother to let her dress as a boy so that she could go to university. "I thank God for willing that it be turned to letters and not another vice," Juana wrote of her passion for learning, "for it was practically unconquerable."[18] As a child, she was so devoted to her studies that she even abstained from cheese, as she had heard a rumour that it dulled the mind.

When Juana turned 12, she was sent to Mexico City to enter the service of Vicereine Leonor Carreto, the wife of the 33rd Viceroy of New Spain. Her intellect was deemed so impressive that the viceregal couple arranged for Juana to be tested by the city's leading scholars. She apparently sailed through her interview "like a royal galleon defending itself against a few rowing boats".[19] Juana's fame grew as the Vicereine's lady-in-waiting, but the pleasures of the court – and having to turn down several marriage proposals –

evidently wore thin. Four years later, she took her vows, and she lived within the walls of the Convent of San Jerónimo for the rest of her life.

In the convent, Juana was free to read and write as she pleased. Unlike other nuns, she did not live under a vow of poverty, and was able to amass a huge library of four thousand texts – thought to be the greatest in all of Mexico. She even turned her convent's *locutorio* – the room where nuns were able to meet with outsiders behind an iron grille – into a salon where she entertained other intellectuals and scholars.

And she wrote and wrote – plays and essays and poetry, including poems of great love and feeling for two Vicereines, Leonor Carreto and María Luisa Manrique. When Juana heard of Leonor's death, she wrote in "Sonnet 187":

She was born where the east draws a scarlet veil

at the rising of the rubicund star,

and she died where, with burning, ardent desire

the depths of the sea swallows that red light;

for it was needed for her divine flight

that like the sun she travel around the world.[20]

Scholars still debate whether Juana meant such verse romantically, but one thing is for sure – she felt a far stronger affinity with women than men, and sometimes that passion exploded with more erotic sentiment than intellectual appreciation. For example, in "Redondilla 87", she wrote admiringly of a woman named Feliciana:

I shall not play the slenderness

of your fine, exquisite torso

for the bend of your waist is as

troubling as a trill in the song.[21]

By 1690, Juana was already being called The Phoenix of Mexico and The Tenth Muse – presumably after Sappho (*see* page 14) – and hailed as one of the New World's greatest intellectuals. That year, she wrote a private letter that critiqued a famous Jesuit priest's sermon. It would later prove to be her death warrant. The Bishop of Puebla, Manuel Fernández de Santa Cruz, began circulating it without her consent, complete with a disparaging preface that he had written under a female pseudonym, Sor Filotea de la Cruz.

"Sor Filotea" criticized Sor Juana's intellectual pursuits, and Juana came back swinging – in "Respuesta a Sor Filotea" ("Response to Sister Filotea"), she put forth a defence of not only her own intellect, but the intellect of her gender, placing herself within a lineage of educated women, from Hypatia to Christina, Queen of Sweden. "I do not study to write, much less to teach (which would be excessive pride in me), but only to see whether by studying I will be less ignorant,"[22] she cried, adding, "How, without great knowledge of the rules and parts that constitute history, can the historical books be understood?"[23]

This proto-feminist manifesto was Sor Juana's great downfall. She had overstepped the mark so severely that clerics even started blaming her for natural disasters. The Church forced her to dismantle her beloved library and barred her from publishing, and in 1694 she was made to repent further by signing in her own blood a reaffirmation of faith. The last thing that The Tenth Muse of Mexico wrote was in her convent's Book of Professions, shortly before she fell ill and died during an epidemic: "In this place is to be noted the day, month, and year of my death...I, worst of all the world, Juana Inés de la Cruz."[24]

CAI YAN

nown in China as a "phantom poet"[25], most of the work of Cai Yan (also known as Cai Wenji, *c.* 2nd century–3rd century AD) has vanished, and her three surviving poems are the subject of much controversy. Precious little remains of this woman, said to have been so clever that she could remember and write out the contents of 400 scrolls.

Her poetry shows the agony of losing one's place in the world and the struggle to adapt in a strange, foreign land. What we do know of Cai Yan's life suggests a tormented existence. She married at 16, only to become unexpectedly widowed. Soon after, her father Cai Yong, a well-known scholar and advisor to the ruling warlord, found himself victim of an armed insurrection and was condemned to prison.

As the region slid into chaos, Cai Yan was abducted by soldiers as a prisoner of war and palmed off on the Xiongnu, a band of nomadic tribes from the steppes of Central Asia, and taken to their land in the north. In the two poems of "Beifen Shi" ("Poems of Lament and Resentment"), Cai Yan records the horror of her kidnapping and of being towed through a country scarred by massacre and war:

Wherever they went, everything was destroyed.

None survived the slaughter,

Corpses and skeletons propped each other.

On their horses' flanks they hung the heads of men,

On their horses' rears they carried off women.[26]

The captives were beaten by their guards, and they barely dared to speak to each other. Their suffering was great, as the poems reveal:

By day we traveled wailing and weeping,

By night we sat lamenting and moaning.

We wished for death but could not get it,

We wished for life but had no chance.

What have we done against blue Heaven

To encounter this calamity?[27]

Once she entered Xiongnu-held territory, she was hostage in a "border wasteland"[28] made all the more alien by her grief. She was forced to marry a tribal chieftain, the second-in-command to the Xiongnu ruler. Cai Yan languished there for twelve years, bearing him two children whom she grew to love regardless. Sometime around AD 206, the ruling warlord Cao Cao – a great admirer of Cai Yan's father – decided to ransom Cai Yan for a huge sum of jade and gold and bring her home.

The cost was dear – Cai Yan had to leave behind her young children. They begged her to stay:

The children came forward and embraced my neck,

They asked: "Where are you going, Mother?

They say Mother is to go away,

How can you ever come back?

Mother has always been loving and kind,

Why do you now become unkind?

We are not yet grown up,

What shall we do if you don't care for us?"

The sight of this collapsed my innards,

My confusion grew to madness.

I wailed and wept, caressed them with my hands[29]

Cai Yan returned to China under the protection of Cao Cao and was given in marriage to Dong Si, one of the ruler's military commanders. But her homecoming was bittersweet – thanks to the decade she had spent abroad, she was deemed neither Chinese nor Xiongnu, and her second marriage had conclusively tainted her in the eyes of her kin. As the Tang dynasty historian Liu Zhiji (*fl.* 8th century) sniffs: "Dong's wife, née Cai, gave birth to barbarian children and was shamed in an alien court. Of literary merit she had more than enough, but her moral behavior was defective. This is an instance of words and actions contradicting each other."[30]

Still, Cai Yan found favour with Cao Cao because of her eloquence and learning. When her husband was sentenced to death, the official history of the Eastern Han dynasty *Hou Han Shu* describes Cai Yan storming the royal court to plead for mercy. When Cao Cao regretfully informed her that the execution order had already gone out, she swayed him with the words: "Your Honour has thousands of horses in his stable and gallant soldiers by the hundreds to do his bidding. Would you not spare one man and a fast horse to save a person from imminent death?"[31]

Her only attributed works in existence are the two poems of "Beifen Shi" in *Hou Han Shu*, and "Hujia Shiba Pai" (Song of the Barbarian Reed-Whistle in Eighteen Stanzas), recorded in an 11th-century anthology. One Sui dynasty (AD581–618) historian recounts that there was a *Collected Works of Cai Wenji*, but this has since been lost.

Scholars are still locked in bitter disagreement over the authorship of the Cai Yan poems. Some believe that only one of the poems in "Beifen Shi" was written by Cai Yan; others claim that only two out of the three are legitimate. There is even a school of thought that holds that none of the poems can be truly Cai Yan's, and that they were written by impersonators who appropriated her story in verse. The debate grew so loud that an academic volume from 1959 had no less than 29 essays arguing both for and against the authenticity of the poems. Like her Greek compatriot Sappho (*see* page 14), we can only glean what we know of Cai Yan from fragments passed down through history.

ometime in the 1930s, a reporter covering an Indian pro-independence protest was startled to see a middle-aged woman in a rocking chair on a street corner, serenely watching the end of the march. This was Sarojini Naidu (1879–1949) – poet, freedom fighter and future governor of Uttar Pradesh – and she was waiting for the police to cart her off to jail.

Born in Hyderabad, Sarojini Naidu grew up in the kind of family where it wasn't unusual for the children to learn multiple languages and dialects – her elder brother, Virendranath, apparently spoke 16. But as a child, there was one language that Sarojini refused to learn: English. Her father – who had taught himself Sanskrit, Greek and Hebrew for fun – was infuriated. He locked her in her bedroom until she proved that she could write a stanza in the language. It may sound especially harsh by today's parenting standards, but it clearly ignited something in Sarojini, and it set her off on a journey that would see her affectionately called The Nightingale of India by much of the country, including Mahatma Gandhi himself.

As a teenager, Sarojini begun to toy with poetry and drama in multiple languages. When her father passed a copy of her Persian play *Maher Muneer* to the Nizam of Hyderabad, it was enough for the ruler of the state to pay for the then-16-year-old to study overseas – first at King's College London and then at Girton College, University of Cambridge. Her mentor at Cambridge, the literary critic Edmund Gosse, read her English poetry and professed himself dismayed at Sarojini's "anglicizing her feelings"[32] with references to the English countryside and churches. In order to find her place in literature, he urged, Sarojini had to become "a genuine Indian poet of the Deccan".[33]

In 1898, Sarojini returned to India to marry her childhood sweetheart. She published her first book of poetry, *The Golden*

Threshold, to critical acclaim seven years later. It seemed that Sarojini had finally found her voice back in India, where she wrote eloquently of its palanquin bearers and snake charmers, praising its henna and traditional dances, and describing the beauty of nightfall in her birthplace of Hyderabad. She dedicated it to Edmund Gosse.

At the same time, India's long-simmering independence movement was starting to boil over, and Sarojini threw herself into the action with the same vigour that she applied to poetry. She struck up a close friendship with independence leader Gopal Krishna Gokhale, who advised her to turn her talent for words into something that could rouse the masses into joining their cause. "After each meeting," Sarojini later said, "I would carry away the memory of some fervent and stirring word of exhortation to yield my life to the service of India."[34] In 1914, the ailing Gopal passed away. His final words to her were: "If you live, remember that your life belongs to India. My work is done."[35]

That same year, in a shabby house in West London, Sarojini met Gandhi for the first time. Already famous for his campaign against racism in South Africa, he was sitting on the floor and eating tomatoes out of a wooden bowl, a prison-issue blanket wrapped around him. "I burst into happy laughter at this amusing and unexpected vision of a famous leader,"[36] she recalled later.

It launched one of the most affirming friendships of Sarojini's life and was the making of her political career. Sarojini was at the front of the famous Salt March in 1930, marching for 24 days to protest against the British tax on salt production, and she was jailed alongside Gandhi and other political leaders.

Heeding Gopal's words, she began to blend her poetry and public speaking into a uniquely soul-stirring mix. At one meeting of the Indian National Congress in 1915, Sarojini performed the poem "Awake" – an urgent call for Indians of all faiths to come together to protect their mother country:

Hindus: Mother! the flowers of our worship have crowned thee!

Parsees: Mother! the flame of our hope shall surround thee!

Mussulmans: Mother! the sword of our love shall defend thee!

Christians: Mother! the song of our faith shall attend thee!

All creeds: Shall not our dauntless devotion avail thee?

Hearken! O Queen and O goddess, we hail thee![37]

Sarojini went on to publish three more volumes of poetry, dedicating one of them, *The Broken Wing*, to her country and "to the dream of today and the hope of tomorrow".[38] When India won its freedom, she fought for women's suffrage to be included in the new constitution, and was appointed the first female governor of the United Provinces (now Uttar Pradesh).

She remained humble about her literary contributions, describing them as "tinkling little verses".[39] At Sarojini's memorial service, however, Jawaharlal Nehru, the first prime minister of India, gave a fitting tribute to the poet and patriot. "After being drawn into the national struggle," he said, "she did not write much poetry with pen and paper. But her whole life became a poem and a song. And she did that amazing thing – she infused artistry and poetry in our national struggle."[40]

VALENTINE PENROSE

alentine Penrose (1898–1978) was called many things in her time. The poet–artist's ex-husband, the English artist Roland Penrose, once called her "a goddess of the irrational";[41] London's esoteric bookshop Treadwell's described her as an "occultress of Surrealism".[42] But, as one biographer puts it simply, Valentine most of all "liked to think of herself as a witch".[43] And magic did seem to run in her work, which brooded on mysticism and female sexuality with Gothic delight.

Born to a military family in provincial France in 1898, Valentine rebelled against her upbringing, a rebellion that included a failed runaway attempt to join the Folies Bergère cabaret. At 26, she met Roland while visiting a mutual friend in Cassis, a fishing village in the south of France. They married a year later in her hometown, where Valentine scandalized the locals by wearing a sari to the ceremony.

Valentine and Roland leaped into the Surrealist scene of the 1920s, with Valentine writing poetry and novels, and producing intricate collages to accompany her poetic work – images of doll-like Victorian women clutching each other against roiling clouds and jagged mountain peaks. In Egypt, she studied the occult and esoteric religion under a Cuban-born mystic called Count Galarza de Santa Clara. In *Herbe à la lune* ("Moonlight Grass"), her first book of poetry, she combined nature and the feminine, as in the poem "There Is the Fire":

There is the fire it burns and I am the water I drown

o icy girl

Earth is my friend

also the moon her servant

thus we meet at the end of our caverns[44]

Many Surrealists proclaimed the age of man to be over; women were seen as being much closer to the subconscious mind that the movement so prized, or, as the Surrealist writer and poet André Breton declared in 1945: "The time should come to assert the ideas of woman at the expense of those of man, the bankruptcy of which is today so tumultuously complete."[45] Unfortunately, this didn't necessarily translate to success or renown for many female Surrealists, Valentine included, even though Paul Éluard – now seen as one of the founders of the movement – praised her poetry as "poetically limpid, a fleet language, escaping reflection".[46]

But Valentine was growing distant from her husband and the cultural movement he was so invested in. Roland, complaining of their sexual incompatibility, cheated on Valentine on a visit to London, and Valentine herself increasingly preferred the company of women. (Years earlier, Valentine had even attempted to seduce Roland's sister-in-law, Bertha, by climbing into her bed in Cassis at 3am. "She was in my bed immediately kissing and caressing," Bertha recalled. "I was taken aback, but could not resist. Her clever fingers were everywhere..."[47]) Some believe that Valentine was already having an affair of her own with the French poet and painter Alice Rahon Paalen, with whom she travelled to India.

As Valentine spent more and more time in India, where Galarza was teaching Arabic philosophy, she grew increasingly contemptuous of Surrealism's pretensions and frustrated with their treatment of women. In a sharply worded letter to Roland, Valentine wrote: "Don't tell me that my 'mysticism' tears us apart. It's because you removed me away from you without pity that I went higher, because you proved to be a ghost of narrow human joy..."[48]

Their time apart proved to have a liberating effect on Valentine, who wrote increasingly on lesbian themes and doused them with fragrant references to witchcraft and the occult. In 1937, Valentine published two more volumes of poetry, *Sorts de la lueur* ("Glimmering fates") and *Poèmes*. After the couple's divorce went through in 1939, she followed this several years later with *Martha's Opera*, a neo-Gothic novel that takes place through the letters of two star-crossed female lovers. "Life is only your absence from mine, or mine from yours, since that day, when, as our shawls entangled before the imminent storm, we delayed among the scorched rocks and black thorn bushes,"[49] one protagonist writes to another.

Valentine reconciled with Roland and lived with him and the photographer Lee Miller, his new wife, at their houses in London and Sussex. In a maternal moment, she read their Tarot cards for good luck before Lee gave birch to their son – though her seduction of women continued apace. In *Dons des Féminines* ("Gifts of the Feminine"), her 1951 book of poetry, she puts a lesbian twist on a ceremonial dance performed during marriage:

Beware of women whose sisters are beautiful

Beware of daughters who have beautiful wives

In the crowd where our eyes

Make their barren exchanges.

Zambra the Zambra you my upright wife.[50]

For Valentine, who had gone from wife and muse to poet and artist in her own right, there could be no more beautiful ritual.

MARIANNE MOORE

arianne Moore (1887–1972) was outraged when her first collection, *Poems*, was published in 1921. It was not the reaction one would expect from a poet making her debut – especially not when the poet H.D. (*see* page 65) and her wealthy lover Bryher had financed the book after falling in love with Marianne's work. But Marianne's standards were exacting, and the 34-year-old poet did not think it was to her "literary advantage"[51] to put anything out yet. H.D. and Bryher went ahead anyway.

Although their help with publication was unwanted, their enthusiasm does indicate just how highly Marianne's work was regarded by others. In a generation of great Modernist poets, she was considered one of its greatest and most eclectic. Three years after *Poems*, Marianne produced her first sanctioned volume of poetry, *Observations*, and became the second-ever poet to win the leading avant-garde journal *The Dial*'s $2,000 cash prize for "service to letters"[52] – the first had been T S Eliot. The poet John Ashbery, who went on to win a Pulitzer Prize, said that he was "tempted to call her our greatest Modern poet".[53]

Marianne was born in Kirkwood, Missouri, in 1887. She did not have a typical upbringing – her father had gone insane after a failed business scheme, leaving her mother to raise Marianne and her brother. Some believe that Marianne's mother, Mary Warner, was a closeted lesbian who found love in a relationship with Mary Norcross, a younger woman and suffragist.

Either way, Mary Norcross was the one who nudged Marianne into applying to Bryn Mawr College, and her earliest work appeared in the literary magazines at the women's college. Marianne found the study of science "exhilarating"[54] and

43

even considered studying medicine. "Precision, economy of statement, logic employed to ends that are disinterested, drawing and identifying, liberate – at least have some bearing on – the imagination, it seems to me,"[55] she once said in an interview.

Marianne's poetry was as fastidious and precise as a pipette dropper, each word administered with utmost care. In "Picking and Choosing", she writes: "Literature is a phase of life: if / one is afraid of it, the situation is irremediable; if / one approaches it familiarly, / what one says of it is worthless."[56] She delighted in describing animals – obscure ones like the jerboa, or extinct ones like the rhea – using them as stand-ins for people, places and herself. When she climbed Mount Rainier, Washington state, in 1920 with her brother, she compared its glacier to a "glassy octopus symmetrically pointed, / its claw cut by the avalanche".[57]

Observations was greeted rapturously by critics and Marianne's contemporaries, but almost 20 years went by without another volume appearing. She edited *The Dial* for four years, but she remained an enigma even to her closest peers, and her relationship with her mother soured into something downright toxic. Marianne had moved in with her distraught mother after Mary's relationship with Norcross broke down, and the mother and daughter slept in the same bed for almost three decades, renting dismal apartments in New Jersey and New York. Mary restricted Marianne's diet (one Thanksgiving meal consisted of sardines), took over her correspondence, siphoned her earnings into a separate savings account and even edited her daughter's own poetry. A mystified William Carlos

Williams called it her "mother thing";[58] understandably, Marianne never found the time to date or marry.

At the age of 60, Marianne suddenly found a new lease of life when her mother died – and the world sat up and took notice. She even became an unexpected celebrity. *Life* magazine called her the "Leading Lady of US verse";[59] she went on the *Tonight Show*, threw the inaugural baseball to open the new Yankee Stadium, frequented fashion shows and parties, and was profiled by every publication going. "I'm good-natured, but hideous as an old hop toad. I look permanently alarmed, like a frog," she told one journalist. "Well, I do seem at least to be awake, don't I?"[60]

Her career choices grew increasingly eclectic; she came up with the liner notes for Muhammad Ali's spoken word album, and even accepted a job to name Ford's latest series of cars. (Ford rejected her suggestions of Mongoose Civique and Bullet Cloisonné, and called it the Edsel instead.) She remained just as idiosyncratic when it came to her own work, cutting her poetry and editing them down until, sometimes, only three lines remained.

In 1951, *Collected Poems* received the Pulitzer Prize for Poetry. In her seventies – free of her mother and the Modernist movement that birthed her – she finally seemed to have hit her groove: "When it comes out right, it's never from being planned that way," she said of her work. "In fact the only reason I know for calling my work poetry at all is that there is no other category in which to put it. I'm a happy hack as a writer."[61]

When you think of Japanese poetry, what comes to mind is probably classical *waka* poetry of the highly structured haiku kind. But for a brief flowering in the 1930s, there was one writer who spoke in a clear and resonant voice that was light years ahead of *waka*. Sagawa Chika (1911–1936) is now described as Japan's first female Modernist poet, though her work languished unloved for decades.

Sagawa was born Kawasaki Ai in 1911, in the northern rural hinterland of Yoichi, Hokkaido. A sickly child who struggled with her eyesight, Sagawa defied her family as soon as she turned 17 and set off for Tokyo. Her half-brother, Kawasaki Noboru, had made the 1,073-km (667-mile) trip to the metropolis long before, and he had already found his feet in the emerging literary circles of Tokyo.

Sagawa didn't intend to miss out. Her memories of childhood, however, never left her poetry – nor did she fail to observe the drastic difference between countryside idyll and bustling metropolis. "Backside" notes:

Night eats color,

Flower bouquets lose their fake ornaments.

Day falls into the leaves like sparkling fish

And struggles, like the lowly mud,

The shapeless dreams and trees

Nurtured outside this shriveled, deridable despair.[62]

After the Great Kantō earthquake of 1923 left Tokyo in ruins, the city had responded with new vigour and hope. There was jazz in its clubs and avant-garde art journals on the bookshelves. Its streets were full of new buildings and new ideas; men and women ditched their kimonos for Western dress. By the time Sagawa joined her brother, poetry was swept up in this new wave of culture, too. She and her peers abandoned the formalism of *waka* and began writing in free verse. She took her pen name Sagawa from the Japanese characters for "left" and "river" – a possible reference to the Left Bank in Paris, home to writers like Gertrude Stein and Ernest Hemingway – and dreamed of opening a bookstore in the Ginza district of Tokyo, just as Sylvia Beach had done with Shakespeare & Company on the Left Bank in 1919.

Sagawa's first published work was a translation of *Ulysses* by James Joyce, the writer that Sylvia herself had championed, followed by Sagawa's own poetry in *Shi to Shiron* ("Poetry and Poetics"), the magazine that was the beacon of Japan's new Modernist movement. Unlike other female poets of the time, her poetry was not sensual or overtly autobiographical; she communicated through precisely weighted and profound imagery, such as that used in the poem "Ocean Angel":

I wait for the return of those who sleep.

Music marks the bright hour.

I try to protest, raising my voice –

The waves come erase it from behind.

I was abandoned in the ocean.[63]

Sagawa became one of the most prominent voices in the Arcueil Club, a society of avant-garde poets best known for producing the literary journal *Madame Blanche*. But disaster struck in 1935 when doctors told her that she was in the advanced stages of stomach cancer. "People are putting aside their work to attend to me, and yet I feel like my illness is not my own," she wrote in her diary, one of the last things she published. "I just don't feel like I own it. I want to get better quickly. I want to eat dinner together at the small table in our house in Setagaya."[64]

Sagawa never returned to her home in Setagaya. She was only 24 when she died, and Japanese literature lost its new-found freedom under an increasingly censorious nationalist government. The country's avant-garde poets were terrified into submission by the Special Higher Police (also known as the Thought Police), a fearsome bureau that sought to investigate and arrest subversive elements in the country.

Even after the end of World War II, Japan continued to reject poetry that was seen as too Western, and Sagawa's work fell through the cracks. She had only ever printed 350 copies of a single volume of poetry, one of which was fortuitously discovered in the 2000s by translator Sawako Nakayasu. Dedicating her translation to Sagawa herself, Nakayasu wrote in its preface: "I have heard her referred to as everything from 'a minor Modernist' to 'everybody's favourite unknown poet' – I would be curious to see how these labels change over time."[65]

ANNA AKHMATOVA

nna Akhmatova (1889–1966) described herself as a Cassandra – doomed to prophesy and pay witness to the events that befell her beloved country in the 20th century. She was born in 1889 into the echelons of the Russian upper classes – her father was a proud navy man and her mother was from one of Kiev's richest landowning families. By the age of 11, Anna had written her first poem – only to be told off by her father for being a "decadent poetess".[66] It prompted her to take a pen name to avoid embarrassing her family: Akhmatova, in honour of a supposed Tartar ancestor.

Anna grew to be a towering 180cm (5ft 11in) tall, and she possessed elegance, charisma and humour in spades; men and women flocked to be at her side. Her first husband, fellow poet Nikolai Stepanovich Gumilev, was driven to attempt suicide when she first rejected him. On Nikolai and Anna's honeymoon in Paris, the painter Amedeo Modigliani met Anna and he, too, fell madly in love with her, drawing her no less than 16 times. In one 1912 poem, she wrote fondly of her time with Modigliani:

When you're drunk it's so much fun –

Your stories don't make sense.

An early fall has strung

The elms with yellow flags.[67]

Though Anna visited him a year later on her own, the affair was short-lived, and she soon returned to her husband. The couple became leading lights in the revolt against symbolism and were key figures in Acmeism, a movement in poetry that stressed clarity and straightforwardness. Anna transfixed the literary circles of St Petersburg with her poetry; at the Stray Dog cabaret and poetry salons, Anna, in between cigarettes, read out her poetry to an adoring audience.

As the Great Terror took hold in the 1930s, Anna began secretly composing her great epic poem *Requiem 1935–1940* during the 17 months she spent with countless other families outside Moscow prison, waiting for news of their incarcerated children. The lament was published in 1962 in Munich, with the disclaimer that it was without the consent of its author:

No, not under alien heavens,

And not by alien wings preserved,

At that time I was with my people,

Where, alas, my people were.[73]

Anna's fortunes wavered through the coming decades. Her first volume of poetry in years, *From Six Books*, was published in 1940, only for Stalin to withdraw it from the shelves. Lev was imprisoned again, and desperation drove Anna to write several poems that praised the state, hoping that it would be enough to secure his release – it wasn't. The 1950s and 1960s brought better luck; Lev was freed and Anna was able to publish several books. Two years before her death, she was even allowed to travel to Italy to receive the Etna Taormina International Prize in Poetry. Her homeland, however, took a while longer to come around to Anna – it was two more decades until her entire body of work was finally made available.

By the time she died of heart failure in 1966, Anna Akhmatova had survived two revolutions and several wars, and had endured years of state censorship and repression. Her books had been pulped and suppressed, her son had spent years in the gulag and she had been scorned by Andrey Zhdanov, Stalin's head of cultural policy, as "half nun, half whore".[74] But even as her literary peers were fleeing Russia, she had never abandoned her beloved country.

i n 1936, June Jordan's (1936–2002) mother had a dream while she was still months from giving birth to her. She "had been visited in her sleep by angels who had told her that this first-born would prove to be a great help to her people: Colored people," June recalled in her autobiography. "She was being blessed."[75]

June did turn out special, or, in the author and poet Alice Walker's words: "June Jordan makes us think of Akhmatova, of Neruda. She is the bravest of us, the most outraged...She is the universal poet."[76] Over the course of her life, June wrote verse, plays, essays, books and even opera librettos. When she wasn't marching or speaking out against injustice, she was writing about it – she apologized in verse on behalf of America for its treatment of Lebanon's Palestinian refugees, and she wondered what it would take to reduce police brutality. "Poem about Police Violence" queries: "Tell me something / what you think would happen if / everytime they kill a black boy / then we kill a cop[...] / you think the accident rate would lower subsequently?"[77]. In essays, she addressed everything from O J Simpson to Islam, and from black feminism to bisexuality.

Born in Harlem, New York, to two West Indian immigrants, June was a precocious and gifted child who began writing poetry at the age of seven. Her father had wanted a son, but he settled for turning June into a perfect student, drilling her in Shakespeare and arithmetic, and using his belt on her when she fell short. "I would become that sturdy, brilliant soldier, or he would, well, beat me to death,"[78] June wrote. Her mother suffered from severe depression and eventually took her own life, which June was deeply affected by and that served to cement her feminism. In her essay "Many Rivers to Cross" she writes,

"I came too late to help my mother to her feet. By way of everlasting thanks to all the women who have helped me to stay alive I am working never to be late again."[79]

Her parents sent her to all-white prep schools before she went to Barnard College, where her already-present alienation was compounded by the college's all-white syllabus. At a time when interracial marriage was frowned upon – and even illegal in some places – she married a white student, though the relationship did not last and she was left to raise her son on her own.

In 1969, she published her first poetry collection, *Who Look at Me*, written in what she called Black English (June hated the word Ebonics, but nevertheless saw the vernacular as a vital part of African–American identity). She filed stories for the *New York Times* and taught at universities like Yale and the University of California, Berkeley, where she pioneered a programme called Poetry for the People. Under June's tutelage, graduates were trained to go into the local community to teach poetry as a means of empowerment – everywhere from prisons to high schools and churches. As one former student put it, June showed that poetry was not "some high language that you trade in high buildings. It's about creating ideas to envision and create a better place."[80]

Who Look at Me was followed by over two dozen more books and collections of poetry, in which she explored notions of identity and liberation, and her own sexuality. "Bisexuality means I am free and I am as likely to want and to love a woman as I am likely to want and to love a man, and what about that?" she wrote. "Isn't that what freedom implies?"[81]

One writer described her as a master of "stitching together the personal and political so the seams didn't show"[82] – the struggles of the oppressed and vulnerable were her struggles, too, though she was always careful to acknowledge her own privilege and shortcomings. In *Some of Us Did Not Die*, the 2002 volume of essays she completed shortly before dying of breast cancer, she wrote: "I have evolved from an observer to a victim to an activist passionately formulating methods of resistance against tyranny of any kind. And most important, I think, is this: I have faced my own culpability, my own absolute dirty hands, so to speak, in the continuation of injustice and powerful intolerance."[83]

June also offered a simple but radical solution to prejudice: love and hope. After the Harlem race riot of 1964, in which a 15-year-old African–American boy was shot by police in front of his school friends, she sold a story to *Esquire* magazine with her mentor, the architect Buckminster Fuller, envisioning a redesign of her old neighbourhood – spiralling towers of "beautiful and low-cost shelter"[84] overlooking communal spaces and green parks, a kind of "federal reparations to the ravaged peoples of Harlem".[85]

She called it "Skyrise for Harlem"; *Esquire*'s editors dismissed it as hopeless utopianism and entitled it "Instant Slum Clearance" in print. June begged to differ. She loved her community, and she loved Harlem. Like her mother dreaming of her unborn daughter, June dreamed of an America that was more equal and loving than the country that came before.

"I think of myself as a political person doing whatever I do, but basically what I aim for is to make love a reasonable possibility...it's that possibility that makes living worthwhile," she said in an interview. "My commitment to love is not an alternative to my political commitments. It's the same thing."[86]

hen Salomé Ureña (1850–1897) was born in the Dominican Republic in 1850, the former Spanish colony had only just wrestled its independence back from neighbouring Haiti six years previously. The struggles of the fledgling country clearly left their mark on a young Salomé, who grew up to be the first Dominican national poet. But, as it turns out, the story is far more complicated than that of your average freedom-loving patriot.

Salomé's parents traced their ancestry back to two of the Caribbean country's most distinguished families. Her father, Nicolás Ureña de Mendoza, was an eminent poet, politician and lawyer, and her mother, Gregoria Díaz de León, came from landowning aristocratic stock. Nicolás made sure that his bright young daughter was taught classics, English and French literature, and even botany. Salomé immediately took to poetry, and began publishing her work at the age of 17 – first under the pen name of Herminia, and then under her full name.

Herminia née Salomé was a sensation. Once the local newspapers started printing her poetry, overseas newspapers expressed interest in the Dominican Republic's newest literary wunderkind. "To the Fatherland" was one of her earliest works:

Tear off, my homeland, the cloak that

barbaric cruelty placed over your shoulders;

lift your bloodied forehead from the dust,

and sing the saintly hymn of union and liberty.[87]

Her poetry offered a battle cry for a young country anxious about its status in the world, and praised the virtues of progress, freedom and enlightenment. Young Dominicans learned her words by heart, and her verses even appeared as graffiti on the walls of Santo Domingo, the capital city. By the time she turned 28, she was presented with a public medal on account of her literary work.

In 1880, Salomé married Francisco Henríquez y Carvajal, a doctor, intellectual and public figure who would later become president of the country. It was also the year when she published her first volume of poetry, *Poesías* ("Poetry"), which contained her epic poem *Anacoana* – named after the indigenous female Taíno chief who was cruelly murdered by Spanish conquistadors. One Dominican contemporary, the writer Federico García Godoy, wrote approvingly of Salomé: "Her poetry is virile and full of greatness, as if composed to the heat of the great ideas of regeneration and progress that the modern spirit continuously spreads to every corner of the globe."[88] In other words, Salomé's verse was good enough to build a republic on. She was seen as an icon of patriotism – aided in no small measure by the fact that she also founded the country's first non-religious school for girls.

But Salomé's own past was also more complex than that of a straightforward revolutionary. Prone to deep episodes of melancholy, she almost never left her house in Santo Domingo. She was twenty-nine when she married Francisco, who was eight years her junior. She was left to raise their three children on her own when he went off to Paris to study medicine, where he had an affair with a French woman and fathered an illegitimate child.

Salomé was tormented by his absence: "I would like to tell you how much I suffer; I would like to tell you that I cannot wait for you with tranquility, because my spirit is no longer strong enough to prolong its torment," she wrote in one letter. "I dreamt with the hope of seeing you within three or four months, and you kill me by telling me that the day we see each other is so distant that it is impossible to set a date. But, my God! I cannot live like this any longer; I am terrified, I am afraid of life, I am afraid of this loneliness in my heart!"[89]

This passion did not just find an outlet in her patriotic verse; it escaped in heartfelt poetry that traded national praise for erotic longing, such as in "Love and Longing", where she writes of Francisco:

I want to tell you that before your gaze

I feel a weak shiver,

that your beloved voice maddens me

that in your smile I live in ecstasy,

that you dominate my whole being."[90]

Nineteenth-century society received these words with unease; Salomé's own son, Pedro Henríquez Ureña, omitted this poem from a later collection of his mother's work.

It was not the only way in which aspects of Salomé's identity were erased. A rare daguerreotype photograph shows that Salomé was of mixed-race heritage, but subsequent portraits have whitewashed her. In one oil painting based on the original daguerreotype, Salomé's features were altered, her hair straightened and her skin lightened. In present-day commemorative monuments and busts of Salomé, the country's first national poet could be thought to be white. Salomé is still remembered and celebrated in the Dominican Republic, but her entirety as a person – her racial identity and her sexuality – is only just beginning to be revealed.

HROTSVITHA OF GANDERSHEIM

he German humanist scholar and poet Conrad Celtes was visiting the Benedictine convent of St Emmeram in the 1490s when he came upon a startling 10th-century codex in its library. It wasn't the Latin verse or its six comedies – all with a strong ecclesiastical bent – that shocked Conrad. It was the fact that the author of the Emmeram–Munich manuscript, as it is now known, was a woman.

Hrotsvitha of Gandersheim (*c.*935–*c.*973), sometimes called Hrosvit, wasn't shy about it. In a Latin pun on her Saxon name, she named herself Clamor Validus ("Forceful Testimony") in her work. She was so remarkable in Celtes's time that he was accused of forgery when he published her work in 1502. In her own time, five centuries previously, her literary gifts must have been seen as extraordinary – even heaven-sent.

That's pretty much what Hrotsvitha thought, too. Little is known about her life prior to entering Gandersheim, a Benedictine abbey in Lower Saxony, but scholars believe that she was of noble Saxon birth and a canoness as opposed to a nun, enjoying relatively greater freedom than her more cloistered sisters. Hrotsvitha emphasizes, however, that she was just as indebted to God as any other person: "I will not deny that through the grace of the Creator I have acquired some knowledge of the arts," she once wrote. "He has given me the ability to learn – I am a teachable creature – yet of myself I should know nothing. He has given me a perspicacious mind, but one that lies fallow and idle when it is not cultivated."[91]

Gandersheim was a bustling centre of political and cultural activity – it even had its own hospital. In 947, Holy Roman Emperor Otto I gave the abbey its independence, meaning that the abbess could run her own court and even raise an army. At Gandersheim, Hrotsvitha received one of the finest educations that a woman of her time could have, and was tutored by the abbess herself, Gerberga II. She was introduced to classical writers Virgil, Ovid and Terence, and was encouraged by Gerberga to write her own religious interpretations of these pagan texts. "There are many

Catholics," Hrotsvitha observed, "and we cannot entirely acquit ourselves of the charge, who, attracted by the polished elegance of the style of pagan writers, prefer their works to the holy scriptures."[92] It was her mission "to glorify, within the limits of my poor talent, the laudable chastity of Christian virgins in that self-same form of composition which has been used to describe the shameless acts of licentious women".[93]

Hrotsvitha, ever the faithful servant of God, was determined to show that Christians could do drama better, and recast saints, martyrs, holy virgins and repentant pagans in the hero role accordingly. In one of her comedic plays, *Dulcitius*, three chaste sisters choose death over dishonour in the form of sex with Dulcitius, the Roman governor of Thessalonica. "I will yield to no man who persuades me to sin,"[94] the youngest declares. The governor's right-hand man shoots her full of arrows instead. Over the course of the story, God's power is revealed in various miracles – first the Romans comically find themselves unable to strip the sisters of their clothes to shame them, and then the two of the sisters remain inexplicably unburned, even when tied to the stake and set afire. Still, all three women choose martyrdom: "We are weary of this world," one says to God, "and we implore Thee to break the bonds that chain our souls, and to let our bodies be consumed that we may rejoice with Thee in heaven."[95]

The tales may have been high-minded in virtue, but Hrotsvitha's tone was always humble, witty and wise. "I strive only, although my power is not equal to my desire, to use what talent I have for the glory of Him Who gave it me," she wrote. "If this pious devotion gives satisfaction I shall rejoice; if it does not, either on account of my own worthlessness or of the faults of my unpolished style, I shall still be glad that I made the effort."[96]

Only six plays, eight legends in narrative verse and two historical works have been discovered so far. Scholars believe it is unlikely that any of her plays were ever staged; they were probably only ever read or recited by other members of her abbey. Today, however, Hrotsvitha is celebrated as Germany's first female poet, and some believe her to be the first female playwright ever recorded. There is even an asteroid named after her – which, given Hrotsvitha's closeness to God, would certainly have pleased her.

H.D.

ears before the birth of H.D. (1886–1961), a fortune-teller told her mother her child would be exceptional. "I often wondered what the fortune-teller told Mama," H.D. wrote in her childhood memoirs *The Gift*. "Mama always said to the university ladies…'It's funny that the children are not gifted.'"[97]

She was wrong, of course. It was H.D. – journeying to London where she helped launch a sensational new poetry movement – who turned out special. In jettisoning the contrived sentimentality of Victorian literature in favour of directness and free verse, Imagism would later be called "the first Modernist literary movement or group in the history of English literature"[98] – and H.D. was its high priestess.

Hilda Doolittle's childhood was spent in Bethlehem, a Pennsylvania settlement founded in 1741 by the Moravian Brethren, a Protestant sect that had fled persecution in Europe for the US. Hilda was raised in the faith, later saying: "I must have the absolutely pure, mystical Moravian pietism or hard-boiled Freudian facts."[99]

Her father was a professor at the University of Pennsylvania, where Hilda met Ezra Pound, a freshman student. They were both 15 and were engaged by 1907; Hilda had already dropped out of Bryn Mawr College with dismal grades. Ezra called her his "dryad" and named her "Saint Hilda" in an early book of his poems entitled *Hilda's Book*. But Ezra had been secretly wooing another woman all throughout the engagement, and he left for Europe in 1908.

Depressed, Hilda observed of her situation: "She was a disappointment to her father, an odd duckling to her mother, an importunate overgrown unincarnated entity that had no place here."[100] Then she met the poet Frances Gregg. Frances was Hilda's first female love, and they called themselves "wee witches".[101] But there was another problem: Frances was simultaneously having an affair with Ezra. In her diary, Frances sums it up thus: "Two girls in love with each other, and each in love with the same man."[102]

Hilda was tormented by this, but never held it against either of them, and in 1911 she travelled to England with Frances and Frances's mother, though the latter two returned home fairly soon. Hilda maintained that Ezra gave her "the jolt that got me out of the University groove, set me with my face toward Europe, eventually led to my staying on in London"[103], and they stayed friends and close collaborators. In London, she met the poet Richard Aldington; they quickly moved in together, living in a flat across the road from Ezra.

The three Imagists were set to kick off their movement and Pound suggested the name H.D. to Hilda. It wasn't long before six of the founding group's poems – three of them signed by "H.D. Imagiste" – were published in the Chicago-based literary journal *Poetry*. Pound's covering letter in submitting H.D.'s verse to the journal's editor said admiringly: "It's straight talk, straight as the Greek!"[104]

World War I brought fresh chaos. In 1915, H.D. suffered a stillbirth, which she blamed on the news of the sinking of the *Lusitania*. Richard enlisted in the army and embarked on an affair with another woman. H.D. reflected on this in her poem "Eros":

Is it bitter to give back

love to your lover

if he wish it

for a new favourite?

who can say,

or is it sweet?

Is it sweet

to possess utterly?

or is it bitter,

bitter as ash?[105]

Meanwhile, H.D. had a child with the English composer Cecil Gray, and then embarked on a new romance, with Winifred Ellerman, a younger, wealthy Englishwoman who greatly admired H.D.'s verse. They travelled and socialized among the literary jet set and, with Kenneth Macpherson (Ellerman's husband and H.D.'s lover), set up a film company called the Pool Group, which published a film journal entitled *Close Up*. They remained in touch, even after Ellerman's two marriages of convenience, and travelled to Sappho's birthplace in Greece together (*see* page 14).

Thanks to a period of psychoanalysis with Sigmund Freud himself, H.D. also found a way to embrace her bisexuality: "I have gone terribly deep with papa [Freud]," she wrote. "He says, 'You had two things to hide, one that you were a girl, the other that you were a boy.' It appears that I am that all-but extinct phenomena, the perfect bi-."[106]

H.D. began to rebel against Imagism, and she eventually broke with the movement completely. Her 1944 sequence of 43 poems *The Walls Do Not Fall* references Egyptian mythology and mysticism; the World War II lament was written as bombs dropped over London, but it simultaneously emphasizes the triumph of art over violence:

remember, O Sword,

you are the younger brother, the latter-born,

your Triumph, however exultant,

must one day be over,

in the beginning

was the Word.[107]

H.D. continued writing through her fifties with her epic poems *Helen in Egypt* and *Trilogy*, and received an American Academy of Arts and Letters medal in 1960. The year after, she suffered a stroke and died. Her headstone aptly takes its words from her 1931 poem "Epitaph":

So you may say,

"Greek flower; Greek ecstasy

reclaims for ever

one who died

following

intricate song's lost measure."[108]

Novelists & Short Story Writers

MURASAKI SHIKIBU

he *Tale of Genji* is remarkable for many reasons. As a book numbering some 1,300 pages in its latest English translation, it weaves an epic tale of Japanese courtly love and palace intrigue across four generations from the Heian-kyō imperial palace in what is now Kyoto. Its transcendent prose has been compared to the greatest literary works of James Joyce and Vladimir Nabokov. The difference, however, is that *The Tale of Genji* was written some thousand years before Joyce or Nabokov ever put pen to paper – and that the life of its author remains shrouded in mystery. Murasaki Shikibu (*c.*973–*c.*1014) isn't even her real name.

What we do know is that during the Heian period (794–1185) in Japan, sometime around 1002 or 1003, an anonymous widow of noble birth picked up a brush and began composing what would later be called the world's first novel. Her actual name was never recorded; Murasaki is the name of *The Tale of Genji*'s heroine, while Shikibu refers to the old government position held by the author's father.

We also know that the woman we call Murasaki was born sometime around 973 into the ruling Fujiwara clan. Both her great-grandfather and her grandfather had work published in the imperial anthology of poetry, but her father had a more lacklustre career, with posts in the provincial backwaters, far from the centre of power in Heian-kyō.

Her intelligence displayed itself early. As a girl, she would listen in on her brother's lessons on Chinese classical texts. "I became unusually proficient at understanding those passages that he found too difficult to grasp and memorize," she wrote in her diary. "Father, a most learned man, was always regretting the fact: 'Just my luck!' he would say. 'What a pity she was not born a man!'"[1]

In 998, Murasaki become one of several wives to a governor who was almost old enough to be her father. They had a daughter, but her husband died in an outbreak of disease, and it is thought that the newly widowed Murasaki began writing *The Tale of Genji* as she mourned her husband. These earliest chapters were so breathtaking that they drew the attention of the imperial court in Heian-kyō, to which she was summoned to attend Empress Shōshi as a lady-in-waiting.

Surrounded by the Heian court in all its fragrant luxury, Murasaki began working in earnest on *The Tale of Genji*. She had plenty of inspiration to draw upon, and a perfect leading man in the form of Genji, her protagonist. *The Tale of Genji* primarily traces his torrid love affairs with women and men, and the chain of events set into motion by this royal playboy, whose beauty is so radiant that he is nicknamed "the shining prince". For contemporary readers, the novel offers a tantalizing window into a bygone period of Japanese history – a time when would-be lovers romanced each other with poetry, and the glimpse of a naked wrist could drive a man mad with lust.

It was a singular piece of work; nothing like it had been written in Murasaki's time, making *The Tale of Genji* a roaring success. Individual chapters were circulated among the court elite like the latest issue of a coveted magazine, and it only grew in stature as the centuries passed. By the Tokugawa, or Edo, period (1603–1868), the marriage dowries of upper-class girls would sometimes even include abridged picture books of *The Tale of Genji* to indicate their status.

It is not clear how or when Murasaki died, though her daughter is known to have lived into her eighties and produced her own collection of poetry. So much from the Heian period has been lost that we are lucky Murasaki's tale survived at all. Today, scholars still pore over *The Tale of Genji* as an early pioneer of the literary novel.

Could Murasaki ever have dared to believe her work could achieve such longevity? In her diary, she writes often of her dissatisfaction and loneliness at court, describing herself as a "retiring old fossil" who is sometimes "vexed at the pettiness of court life", and detailing her worries about what she might have created, if anything, for posterity.

"Here is one who has survived this far without having achieved anything of note. I have nothing in particular to look forward to in the future that might afford me the slightest consolation, but I am not," she added, perhaps with slightly more prescience than she realized at the time, "the kind of person to abandon herself completely to despair."[2]

JAMES TIPTREE JR.

ames Tiptree Jr. (1915–1987) was "a man of 50 or 55, I guess, possibly unmarried...a man who has seen much of the world and understands it well",[3] mused American editor and author Robert Silverberg in his 1975 introduction to Tiptree's anthology of stories *Warm Worlds and Otherwise*. The joke was on Silverberg. Tiptree was, in fact, a 60-year-old woman from Chicago called Alice B Sheldon, who had stolen the name Tiptree from a jar of supermarket jam.

The rest, however, wasn't far off. Alice had travelled widely and lived recklessly; born to an adventurous lawyer who had led three safaris into Central Africa and a glamorous travel writer who could "hike 45 miles up a mountain carrying your rifle and hers",[4] Alice was only six years old when her parents carted her off on dangerous expeditions through Asia and Africa.

Alice rebelled by eloping with the Princeton student seated to her left at her high-society debut. Their marriage lasted six and a half drug-addled and tumultuous years, during which Alice nearly died of an infection following an abortion, was arrested for kicking a police officer in the balls and made several unsatisfying visits to brothels – which proved especially confusing for Alice, who had long suffered unrequited crushes on women. Alice's final word on her first marriage was: "Anyone who shoots a real gun at you when drunk and angry

is simply not husband material, regardless of his taste in literature."[5]

In 1941, she ditched her marriage and came crawling back to her parents, contrite and penniless. A job as the art critic of the newly launched *Chicago Sun* promised some measure of stability, but she ditched that, too, in favour of signing up for the Women's Army Auxiliary Corps. When she got a transfer to the Pentagon as a photointelligence analyst, she challenged her commanding officer, Huntington Denton "Ting" Sheldon, to a game of blindfolded chess, and won. A month later, they were married.

Ting and Alice stayed together for the rest of their lives, but Alice struggled with their sexless marriage, the demands of domesticity and her unresolved sexuality. In her journal, she wrote: "I want, I want, I want, I want. I want to be alone, to be in a crowd, to work, to have children and love them fully, to be fulfilled in body and mind and to carry each of those fulfillments to a point entirely contradictory to all the others."[6]

Alice found her escape in James Tiptree Jr. Science fiction offered her a chance to sublimate everything she felt and thought about gender inequality, her desires for women and her eternal sense of being an outsider. She wrote about humans encountering – sometimes sexually – strange and alien beings, astronauts discovering a world solely populated by women and a reversed alien abduction tale in which the mother and daughter opt to leave Earth behind, despairing of their gender's chances on the planet.

At 51, Alice typed up four stories and sent them off under a Tiptree-signed cover letter. She wanted a pseudonym that was ordinary, commonplace – easy to forget.

To her shock, Condé Nast bought a story; and then sci-fi magazines followed. As Tiptree's reputation grew, Alice began corresponding with fans, editors and authors, including Philip K Dick and Ursula K Le Guin. Ting knew and encouraged her writing, and their marriage deepened over the years: "Since the last 10 years we are so as one it's ridiculous,"[7] she wrote as she turned 65.

The science fiction world was desperate to figure out who Tiptree was, but Alice always rebuffed their attempts. "You know as well as I do we all go around in disguise," she said in a rare interview. "The halo stuffed in the pocket, the cloven hoof awkward in the shoe, the X-ray eye blinking behind thick lenses... So who the fuck cares whether the mask is one or two millimetres thick?"[8]

Alice was finally outed when her mother died. Tiptree had spoken of losing an elderly explorer mother in Chicago, and someone had tracked down the obituary and found Alice listed as the only surviving family member. The revelations seemed to kill some creative spark inside Alice. "I feel as if some microphone had gone dead on me,"[9] she said. She published a novel and a few more short stories, but nothing more.

In 1986, Ting went blind and had a small stroke, and Alice became his full-time carer. Not wanting to die or decline without each other, they had made a suicide pact some years previously, and Alice shot Ting in 1987 as he lay sleeping. Before she turned the gun on herself, she made one final call to their stepson. If she found a way, she promised, she would communicate with him from the next world; a message from the great beyond, just like in one of her stories.

HIGUCHI ICHIYŌ

iguchi Ichiyō (1872–1896) always wanted to be a writer, and a famous one, at that. "Since I was about nine years old, I had loathed to live and die in obscurity," she wrote in her diary. "Day in day out, I wished to surpass others even by an inch."[10]

And her wish was granted. In 2004, the Bank of Japan introduced a new design for the 5,000 yen note. On one side is a spray of fragrant irises; on the other is Higuchi – the Meiji-era author, widely acclaimed in her day.

When Higuchi was born in 1872, Tokyo was still known as Edo and fearsome samurai ruled the land. But as the Meiji period (1868–1912) wore on, Japan was soon turned upside down with the reinstallation of the Emperor and the dismantling of the traditional feudal class system. Higuchi's father, who had worked tirelessly in order to attain the rank of samurai just a few years prior, was forced to take on a low-ranking government post.

The only thing that wasn't changing fast was Japan's treatment of women. They were still treated as the property of their fathers, and then their husbands, and education was low on their list of patriarchal priorities. Higuchi's formal education came to an end just after she topped her elementary school at the age of 12, because, as her mother put it: "Too much education spoils a young girl's future; she should learn sewing and help with the housework."[11]

Her father was unusually enlightened for his time and arranged for her to enter a private girls' school when she turned 14, where she was tutored in traditional Japanese poetry (*waka*) and literature. It was the kind of place where girls turned up for class in lacquered horse-drawn carriages. In her comparatively drab attire, Higuchi began honing her critical powers of

observation, noting of her well-to-do classmates: "I found my old clothes more precious than their damask and brocade, for I found in mine the unfathomable benevolence of my parents and was thoroughly pleased with them."[12]

Disaster befell her family in 1898, when Higuchi was only 17 – her father was struck down by tuberculosis and died shortly after squandering their savings on a failed business venture. Her aging mother and little sister were forced to take on odd jobs as seamstresses and washerwomen. As the sister with the highest level of education, Higuchi suddenly found herself thrust into the position of caretaker and primary breadwinner. It was now imperative that she find a way to make money from her writing, and she set about it with the seriousness of a newly minted head of household, enlisting the help of a novelist and journalist named Nakarai Tōsui. Higuchi sweated over her manuscripts at home only to rip them up in fits of pique – but something in her refused to throw in the towel.

"Perverse as I am, I can't give it up quite so easily, and presumptuously enough I have started writing again," she wrote after one aborted attempt. "I must, by all means, complete it by day after tomorrow. I feel that I will die if I don't finish it. If people wish to laugh at my faint heart, let them laugh."[13]

Success finally came with her novella *Takekurabe* ("Child's Play"), which became a hit when it was published in full in the literary periodical *Bungei Kurabu* ("The Literature Club"). But Higuchi found it difficult to accept praise: "Nine out of ten of the people who come to see me are delighted just to see a woman; they are drawn by the unusual," she said. "That's why even the merest scrap I produce sets them all aflutter."[14]

Higuchi's reticence could also have something to do with the fact that she had sacrificed so much to get to that point. She had developed feelings for Tōsui, but was advised to cut off ties to her mentor or risk besmirching her family's reputation. She had sold almost all her possessions to keep her family afloat; they poured the money into a small convenience store in the red-light district of Yoshiwara, only to watch it fail when a competitor opened on the opposite side of the road.

The street kids who visited Higuchi's shop did, however, provide her with the characters for *Takekurabe*, which follows a group of childhood friends from Yoshiwara as their paths diverge and pull them toward their tragic destinies. Higuchi records their fates with a careful and deeply sympathetic eye, as she does in all her work. She wrote around 20 novellas and short stories, many inspired by the social reality of the red-light district she called home, and often following marginalized women – prostitutes, bar maids, mistresses – attempting to carve out some independence of their own. It was the first time their stories had been told, providing a unique insight into the lives of these people who had been written out of official history.

Higuchi had worked as an author for only five years when she fell sick with tuberculosis – the same illness that killed her father – and she died at the age of 24. She would no doubt be glad to know that her work lives on in Japan's bookshelves and banknotes. As she once wrote, "I do not desire a brocade gown nor am I after a stately mansion. How could I ever stain my name which I wish to leave behind for a thousand years for the sake of temporary gain? I will rewrite even a short story three times, and then I will ask the world to pass judgment."[15]

espite dying at the tender age of 29, Albertine Sarrazin (1937–1967) managed to cram several lifetimes' worth of experience into her short stint on Earth. As a baby, she was Albertine Damien, abandoned and then taken in by social services. When she was a child, she was adopted by a wealthy couple and renamed Anne-Marie. Then there was Albertine the runaway; Albertine the teenage hustler and convicted robber; Albertine the jailbird; and, above all, Albertine the novelist, who wrote gritty tales of life on the margins with all the wit and insight of one who had actually lived it.

Born in Algiers in 1937, Albertine was abandoned by her mother and placed in the care of a retired colonel and his wife. They promptly decamped for Aix-en-Provence, new daughter in tow, but Albertine's bourgeois childhood was shattered when she was raped at the age of ten by a relative. She excelled at school but became a surly, dysfunctional teenager, prone to runaway attempts and arguments, and her parents eventually sent her packing to a reform school in Marseilles.

The Refuge of the Good Shepherd couldn't hold Albertine for long. When she was mid-transit to take an exam at another school, Albertine escaped through the kitchen and hitchhiked her way to Paris. She was joined later by Emilienne, her teenage lover at the Good Shepherd. Destitute and homeless, Albertine turned to sex work and theft to survive. A bungled armed robbery condemned her and Emilienne to jail when she was eighteen – Albertine for seven years, and Emilienne for five. Albertine went on to spend almost a third of her life in and out of various French prisons.

Jail was also where Albertine ended up discovering her literary voice – she wrote her first two novels, *La Cavale* and *Astragal*, behind bars, with *Astragal* written during a four-month jail term for thieving a bottle of whisky from a downtown Monoprix.

Ever the runaway, Albertine had tried to escape her first stint in prison by jumping a 9-m (30-ft) prison wall. She ended up breaking her ankle bone (or, in line with the scientific term that she later adopted as a book title, her astragalus) and was rescued by a passing motorist – Julien Sarrazin, a fellow ex-convict whom she later married.

Albertine immortalizes their meeting in the semi-autobiographical *Astragal*. "Long before he said anything, I had recognized Julien," she wrote. "There are certain signs imperceptible to people who haven't done time: a way of talking without moving the lips while the eyes, to throw you off, express indifference or the opposite thing; the cigarette held in the crook of the palm, the waiting for night to act or just to talk, after the uneasy silence of the day."[16]

Anne, the street-smart and unsentimental protagonist of *Astragal*, spends the rest of the novel on the lam, dogged by paranoia and her memories of prison. "You can't wash away overnight several years of clockwork routine and constant dissembling of self,"[17] Anne thinks to herself as she lands in hospital for her worsening foot. The limb is saved, but Anne suffers the indignity of being treated as Julien's hobbled bit on the side, and dreams of a life beyond petty crime and infidelity: "To have mutilated myself so horribly, to have been so miraculously saved

ALBERTINE
SARRAZIN

vendredi 3 décembre
1976

and put back together, is a sign," she thinks hopefully, "the prelude and the condition of something, a thing much more important than an adulterated love born in jail and half-dead with neglect."[18]

Albertine and Julien's Bonnie and Clyde life of burglaries and incarceration provided more material for her later books. In 1965, she sent the manuscripts for *La Cavale* and *Astragal* to a French publisher, and the two were simultaneously published in October that year. She became a literary sensation and, despite being legally barred from Paris, was granted a special reprieve to do interviews and publicity. Her third novel, *La Traversière*, was published just a year later. It looked as if Albertine had finally orchestrated her most daring escape: leaving behind her years of crime and poverty.

A year before she turned 30, however, a routine kidney operation went hideously wrong and she died on the operating table in Montpellier. Julien successfully sued her doctors and used the damages to create Éditions Sarrazin, a publishing house to make sure that his wife's work was never forgotten. Albertine was later immortalized by the singer-songwriter Patti Smith as "the petite saint of maverick writers", who noted of her brief but luminous life: "She exited the world loved, but also as she had entered it – on a cloud of neglect."[19]

RASHID JAHAN

 n early 20th-century India, good girls were rarely seen and even more rarely heard. Rashid Jahan (1905–1952) – a Communist doctor and author nicknamed the first "angry young woman"[20] of Urdu literature – singlehandedly upended that convention, inspiring a new generation of female writers in the process.

Under the practice of purdah, women from middle- and upper-class families were expected to remain secluded from society and veil themselves in public. Thankfully, Rashid's family was far from conventional. Her father, Sheikh Abdullah, founded their city's first school for Muslim girls and launched the women's magazine *Khatun* ("Woman"), with her mother, Begum Wahid Jahan, as a regular contributor. Despite her liberal upbringing, however, Rashid was still expected to get to her parents' school in a covered palanquin so that no man would lay eyes on her en route.

Rashid left purdah behind when she quit her hometown of Aligarh, Uttar Pradesh, for the Isabella Thoburn College in Lucknow. By the time she studied medicine at Lady Hardinge Medical College in Delhi, she was sporting a radically different look and attitude. The trainee gynecologist had chopped her hair into a chic bob, wore little to no makeup and wasn't afraid to stick up for herself. Her peers and friends adored her for it. "She spoiled me because she was very bold and used to speak all sorts of things openly and loudly, and I just wanted to copy her,"[21] recalls author Ismat Chughtai, who attended school with Rashid. She was a born activist, too – her little sister remembered the staunch nationalist convincing her that wearing Western-style dresses was merely "aping the English rulers who would never consider us their equals".[22]

When Rashid graduated from medical college, she was one of the first Muslim women in India to qualify in medicine. As a loyal Communist, however, Rashid donated her salary to the Party and lived off a rationed allowance. "I'd rather give my time and energy to those who need me and appreciate my services,"[23] she told a friend. Travelling around the north of India to administer to the sick and ailing, she saw the poverty and disease that afflicted her country – especially its women.

Rashid had dabbled in writing at school, but her politics and experience as a doctor translated to her literary work with new-found urgency. As part of what would later become the Progressive Writers' Movement in Lucknow, Rashid wrote in clear-sighted prose and with utter disdain for the status quo. In one story, "Dilli Ki Sair" ("A Visit to Delhi"), a woman in a burqa describes her disgust with male catcallers: "First this damned burqa, then these cursed men. Men are anyway no good but when they see a woman sitting like this they just circle around her. There is no opportunity even to chew paan."[24]

Rashid's boldness landed her in trouble in 1932, when a group of young left-wing authors – of whom Rashid was the only woman – published a provocative collection of short stories entitled *Angarey* ("Burning Coals") that overturned Urdu literary form and set fire to religious and cultural tradition. It outraged all of India. One newspaper declared it "An Absolutely Filthy and Foul Book, or, the Shameless Chronicle of Nameless Hands Which Are Burning with Fire".[25] The Central Standing Committee of the All-India Shia Conference even put out a notice that "the heart-rending and filthy pamphlet...has wounded the feelings of the entire Muslim Community by ridiculing God and His Prophets".[26]

One of the works from *Angarey* that got Rashid into such trouble was *Parde Ke Peeche* ("Behind the Veil"), a short play that horrified people with its candid and no-nonsense depiction of female sexuality. It laments the devastating effect of childbirth on a woman and her marriage: "The truth is that my womb and all the lower parts had slipped so far down that I had to get them fixed, so that my husband would get the same pleasure he might from a new wife."[27]

Rashid's exacting bluntness was meant to puncture the patriarchal attitudes that allowed such suffering to thrive – not that this was appreciated by her intended audience. All four *Angarey* writers were slapped with fatwas, and the uproar from religious clerics pushed the British colonial government into banning the book. Rashid was singled out for particular punishment on account of her gender – she was even threatened with an acid attack.

Rashid only published sporadically after *Angarey* and instead devoted most of her time to medicine. In fact, *Angarey* was almost lost completely when the British authorities destroyed all but five copies. Two were sent to the British Library's Oriental and India Office Collections in London. Some 50 years later they were rediscovered and republished. Her clarion call of righteous anger, however, left its mark on a generation of Urdu writers. As her friend and admirer the writer Ismat Chughtai puts it: "The handsome heroes and pretty heroines of my stories, the candle-like fingers, the lime blossoms and crimson blossoms all vanished…the earthy Rashid Jahan shattered all my ivory idols to pieces."[28]

MARY CARMEL CHARLES

n 1985, a linguistics researcher named William McGregor was working in the Australian beach town of Broome when an old Aboriginal woman approached him with a proposition: would he like to learn her language?

The woman was Mary Carmel Charles (1912–1999), a 73-year-old domestic worker who happened to be one of the last-surviving speakers of Nyulnyul, the Aboriginal dialect spoken by her tribe in the seaside area of Beagle Bay, Kimberley, tucked away in the northwest corner of Western Australia.

Though the Kimberley is roughly the size of Germany, it is known as the outback of the Australian outback for good reason – the land is three times the size of England and is vast, sprawling and sparsely populated. Indigenous Australians lived here for 30,000 years or so until European settlers came calling in the 1890s and settled in Beagle Bay, founding a missionary school run by monks and nuns.

In 1909, three years before Mary's birth and her subsequent arrival at Beagle Bay Mission, the Catholic children's home already had over 110 boys and girls who had been shipped in from all over the Kimberley. At the time, the government policy on indigenous people was one of forced assimilation: Aboriginal and part-Aboriginal children were to be separated from their families and placed in the care of the state, in schools and other institutions where they were barred from speaking their language or practising their culture.

"Generations of Aboriginal women who lived on Beagle Bay Mission have spoken about their deep sense of loss, and their attempts as children to maintain contact with the older people in order to obtain information about the old ways," writes historian Christine Choo. "These attempts were frustrated by the missionaries. Children were not

allowed to talk about their parents or enquire about them. They were forbidden from speaking their own languages, among themselves or with the older people in the colony."[29]

Today, the children who were removed from their own tribes and culture are known as the Lost Generations, and their trauma and anguish were only acknowledged (and apologized for) by the Australian government in 2008. But though Mary was taught by the nuns at the Mission until she was 15, she was brought up by her parents and miraculously clung on to her knowledge of Nyulnyul, carrying it with her 160km (100 miles) down the coast to Broome when she moved there for work. That was where she met William McGregor, then working at the Kimberley Language Resource Centre, which had been set up in 1984 to preserve and transmit Aboriginal languages.

"There's nobody else now who knows the language, only a few, one or two people but they don't know it well. I would like for children to learn Nyulnyul language,"[30] Mary said.

Mary had gone deaf in 1950, but she was determined to find some way of passing the language on. She began a decade-long working relationship with William, in which she sat down with the linguist to begin the slow process of recording her tribe's dialect for posterity. William would write down a sentence in English and show it to Mary, who would then translate it into Nyulnyul for him to note down. The field notes and audio recordings they made are some of the only data in existence on the language.

In 1993, Mary became an author with the children's book *Winin: Why the Emu Cannot Fly*. Translated by William into English and based on a traditional Aboriginal legend passed down from her parents, it tells the Dreamtime story of the emu and the brolga (otherwise known as the Australian crane), and how the emu, the official bird of Australia, ended up with its stumpy wings. Francine Ngardarb Riches, an Aboriginal artist, illustrated Mary's words, and the book was printed in both English and Nyulnyul, with a small translation guide at the back.

In Mary's telling of the myth, the foolish emu flies higher than all other birds, until a jealous brolga tells him that there is a secret to soaring even higher still: shorter wings. The emu – still not exactly the brightest bird in Australia – obediently clips its wings and finds itself unable even to take off, and must now spend its life earthbound.

"I remember when I was young, my parents told me olden-day stories about the emu and a brolga," Mary said when the book came out. "This is just one of the stories and I am glad it is published at last. I'm proud the emu is in a book." She added with evident pride, "I will be eighty-two on the 15th July."[31]

By the time Mary died at the age of 87, the only other fluent speaker of Nyulnyul had died 10 years prior. However, thanks to the efforts of one determined octogenarian, the language lives on in a brightly coloured children's book – proof that literature for the young can be just as historic and meaningful as books for grown-ups.

THERESA HAK KYUNG CHA

 n the opening pages of her novel *Dictée* ("Dictation"), Theresa Hak Kyung Cha (1951–1982) offers her readers a prayer, through words first penned by Sappho (*see* page 14): "May I write words more naked than flesh / stronger than bone, more resilient than / sinew, sensitive than nerve."[32] It's an appropriate epigraph for the Korean–American performance artist's first and only novel, published in the year of her untimely death.

Born in the South Korean city of Busan during the tumult of the Korean War, Theresa was only 12 when her parents decided to uproot the family to Hawaii and then California. South Korea had been left scarred by its brutal war with North Korea, and starvation meant it wasn't unusual for people to resort to foraging wild plants for food. Her family was among the 15,000 or so Koreans who left their homeland to seek a better life in the US.

At the Convent of the Sacred Heart High School in San Francisco, Theresa became fluent in French, the language that peppers *Dictée* alongside English, Latin and Korean. She got a place at the University of California at Berkeley just as second-wave feminism and the student protest movement took off in the 1960s. Theresa studied art and comparative literature, and her knowledge of feminist theory, performance and theatre deepened during the years she spent at Berkeley.

"The main body of my work is with Language, 'looking for the roots of the language before it is born on the tip of the tongue'," she wrote in 1979. "Since having been forced to learn foreign language more 'consciously' at a later age, there has existed a different perception and orientation toward language."[33]

Theresa was specifically interested in the limitations of speech and understanding. Her native Korea had spent the early part of the 20th century gagged under Japanese rule; Korean-language newspapers and magazines had been shut down, students had been taught in Japanese and banned from speaking Korean in school, and any dissent had been mercilessly crushed.

But if Theresa hoped to find herself at home in South Korea, she was sorely disappointed in 1979, when she visited the country for the first time in 16 years with her brother. Too Korean to be truly accepted by America, but too American to pass as Korean, the pair were treated like outsiders and even accused of being spies – just one more layer of confusion and sorrow to add to those already separating Theresa and her supposed motherland.

When Theresa left university, she embarked on an artistic career that spanned performance, film and literature in order to explore the dislocating power of language and place. Her installation and performance work alludes to her fragmented identity; in one performance piece, *Aveugle Voix*, a blindfolded and gagged Theresa unravelled a white banner that began with the message "WORDS-FAIL-ME". In a video and installation piece, *Exilée*, she traced the distance between herself and Korea:

following daylight to the end

of daylight

ten hours twenty three minuits

sixteen hours ahead of this time.[34]

As she entered her thirties, Theresa mused in her notebook: "Thirty – I am not Beethoven. I am not Helen

Keller, Joan of Arc."[35] She was only 31 when her life came to a shocking end. Theresa was en route to meet her husband in Manhattan, where he was photographing the restoration of the Puck Building, a historic property once called the Crown Jewel of SoHo. She was attacked inside by a security guard, who raped her, then strangled and bludgeoned her to death. He was only convicted of second-degree murder and rape five years after the attack.

At the time of her death, *Dictée* had not even been published – Theresa had only just seen the advance copies. The novel is every bit as experimental as her artistic work, its nine sections named after the Greek muses and deploying everything from Roman Catholic prayers, French language exercises and imperial Korean history to archival family photographs. Theresa uses all these to reconstruct the fragmented voices of women lost in time, including Korean revolutionary Yoo Kwan-soon, Joan of Arc and Theresa's mother. The effect is dizzying and mesmerizing, often poetically oblique.

"Dead words. Dead tongue. From disuse. Buried in Time's memory. Unemployed. Unspoken. History. Past. Let the one who is diseuse, one who is mother who waits nine days and nine nights be found. Restore memory. Let the one who is diseuse, one who is daughter restore spring with her each appearance from beneath the earth," she writes. "The ink spills thickest before it runs dry before it stops writing at all."[36]

Dictée lay in obscurity for a decade, before it was reexcavated and hailed by critics as a landmark in Asian–American literature. Though she never lived to see it, Theresa's legacy in both art and literature left its mark. "I saw Cha perform just once, in 1978, at the San Francisco Museum of Modern Art," one *Village Voice* art critic wrote after her death. "At the time I'd never heard the term 'performance art.' Cha gave it indelible meaning."[37]

SAMIRA AZZAM

hen Samira Azzam (1927–1967) died of a sudden cardiac arrest at the age of 39, one of her publishers lamented that she had died of a broken heart. "Azzam's death was not due to a chronic disease but due to the shock she was beaten by," they said. "She died because she was heartily Arabic, because she bore in her heart all the pain and frustration of her nation."[38]

It was the summer of 1967, and Israel had just defeated its Arab neighbours in the Six-Day War, a swift but devastating conflict that expanded its territory and turned more than a quarter of a million Palestinians into refugees. The shock of the defeat prompted Samira to tear up the manuscript for the novel she was working on – her first and only attempt at writing one.

As a teenager in the 1940s, Samira and her family had already fled their home, one family out of the more than 700,000 people who were forced out during the First Arab–Israeli War – an event so cataclysmic that Palestinians call it the Nakba (Arabic for "the catastrophe"). Then, two decades later, Samira watched as history repeated itself.

Born in 1927 to a Christian Orthodox family in Acre, a port city overlooking the Mediterranean Sea, Samira became a schoolteacher at the age of 16 and began writing for a newspaper under the pen name Fatat al-Sahil ("Girl of the Coast"). During the Nakba of 1948, the precocious teenager and her family found themselves refugees in Lebanon. The pain and shock of losing her home never left Samira, and she would revisit Palestine again and again in her stories.

"You ask me how it was [our spring]," she wrote in her final collection of short stories, *Joy Comes From the West*

Window. "And I say as it wasn't in any other place... our spring comes to you carried on clouds of orange fragrance...its fragrance penetrates to you through the sills of the windows, as if you are sleeping on a pillow of perfume...Don't ask me how it was our spring but ask me which spring is comparable to ours."[39]

In 1950, Samira left her family for a job as a school headmistress in Iraq, where she also began apprenticing as a broadcaster for the Near East Arab Broadcasting Company. Eventually, she left teaching and became a full-time radio presenter, and Arab listeners around the region grew to know her voice as she took on jobs at radio stations in Cairo and Baghdad. She also introduced Western authors like Pearl Buck, George Bernard Shaw and John Steinbeck to the Middle East by translating their work into Arabic, and, taking her cue from her days as a teenage columnist, began writing for an Egyptian paper.

In 1954, Samira published her first short story collection, *Tiny Matters*. Her characters reflect the pain and struggle of the Palestinian people; in various incarnations, they are cast out into an unforgiving world, where they are hated and pitied in turn. "There in the village she learns to shed down [her] humanity for loathing...learned to hate... learned revenge,"[40] Samira wrote of one female protagonist, who is disowned by her family after losing her virginity. In another story, "Because He Loves Them", a Palestinian farmer, having "lost self-respect when he lost the land"[41] during the Nakba, is driven to drink and ends up killing his wife in a desolate refugee camp far from home.

In 1959, she was forced to leave Iraq with her husband after the republican regime accused her broadcasts of undermining the government. Once again, Samira found herself without a home. She chose to resettle in Beirut and continued to use her work to call for the homecoming of the Palestinian diaspora. Though she rejected the armed struggle of groups like the Palestine Liberation Organization and advocated diplomacy with neighbouring Arab countries instead, she never gave up on the dream of the Palestinian right of return.

When these allies lost to Israel in 1967, Samira was dismayed. She did not live to see Acre again. But in her six volumes of short stories, she returned again and again to the place where she grew up, "the sweetest of cities"[42] – and she never stopped expressing the hope that the Palestinian people would be able to return home.

"Wipe your tear my brother, it is of no value," she wrote. "Before you is a country waiting... tears will not bring it back and words do not help even when they are sincere and beautiful. Palestine is yearning for your endeavour, for your struggle and your faith."[43]

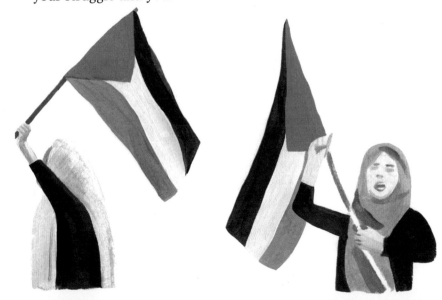

n the early 1940s, Shanghai – once known as the Paris of Asia – was ruled by danger and uncertainty. Its glamorous boulevards were under the control of Japan, and locals had been forced to swap socializing in Art Deco hotels for food shortages and air raids. But the Chinese writer Su Qing, described by one peer as a *luanshi jiaren* ("a beauty at a turbulent time"),[44] didn't just find a way to endure these times – she thrived.

Born in 1914, Su Qing (1914–1982) had always dreamed of getting an education. She was only a freshman at the National Zhongyang University when her parents forced her to drop out and enter an arranged marriage with a man to whom she had been promised when she was 14. The unhappy relationship lasted for ten years before Su Qing filed for separation, taking her two children with her. She entered Japanese-occupied Shanghai society as that rare thing, a divorcee. She was determined to make a living the best way she knew how: writing.

Su Qing's essays, short stories and novels boldly set out to break down conservative gender norms and critique the familial and social forces that had yanked her out of school and yoked her to a man she didn't love. Her efforts won her the admiration of her contemporaries and all of Shanghai. In 1943, she founded her own literary journal, *Heaven and Earth Monthly*, and the accompanying Heaven and Earth Press as a publishing house – the first of its kind run by a young female author. It wasn't long before Su Qing was spoken of in the same breath as the city's greatest actresses and idols, feted in the tabloids and profiled in magazines.

"Some people asked me why I had to write in this war-trodden era?" she said in one postscript to a collection of essays. "Their way of thinking is just the contrary to mine…I know only too well that everything is going to collapse soon, but I

still hope to grasp this moment and seek serenity and fulfillment right away! Otherwise what am I going to do with these few surviving moments?...I want to live, and I want to live in a way that most satisfies myself!"[45]

In 1944, she published her first book, *Jiehun shinian* ("Ten Years of Marriage"), and became a cause célèbre. The semi-autobiographical novel begins on the day of the protagonist's arranged marriage and unspools from there, laying out the various indignities and frustrations of her relationship – including having to pee on her own pillow, as she is barred from leaving her bed until the bridal sedan arrives.

Its dark humour was a stark contrast to the usual overwrought confessional novels of the time, and the bestselling book made her one of Shanghai's most popular writers – but not without controversy. One newspaper branded it pornographic, and a women's magazine accused Su Qing of being a "literary prostitute"[46] bent on "enslaving the minds of Shanghai women and numbing their consciousness of resistance, making people forget oppression and the bloodiness of reality".[47] There were vicious rumours swirling around Su Qing, too – that she secretly supported the Japanese, and that her career was bankrolled by the mayor of Shanghai, who was later executed as a collaborator.

That same year, she wrote an essay entitled "Ziji de fangjian" ("My Own Room") that considered the indignities she endured just for the sin of trying to provide for her own children. "I look around me. I bought everything, even the nails in this room, with my own money," she wrote. "However, what joy can I have in this fact?"[48]

When the Japanese occupation came to an end, Su Qing's connections to the regime, however tenuous, were enough to torpedo her career. Publishers refused to go near her work, and she had to resort to writing under a pseudonym.

Once the Communists took over in 1949, Su Qing managed to find work as a dramatist for local opera and theatre groups under the pen name Feng Yunzhuang, writing historical dramas or adapting traditional Chinese stories for the stage.

In 1955, however, she was arrested on charges of counter-revolutionary behaviour. She had strayed from her job as a faceless, Ministry of Culture-approved scriptwriter to write essays for the *Shanghai Daily* in Hong Kong. Su Qing had stopped short of criticizing the regime – she was too smart for that – but her gentle critique of the new China proved too much for the authorities. That, combined with her old reputation as a sympathizer and her ties to Hu Feng, a literary critic and outspoken critic of Mao, was enough to get her writing banned completely and send her to prison for two years. By the time she was released, the name of Su Qing had faded into obscurity. She died in poverty at the age of 68.

In "Waves", a short story published in 1945, Su Qing seemed to catch a glimpse of the tumult that lay ahead. "Life is like the sea," she wrote, "a vast expanse when calm, aimless, even stymied. Yet when all of a sudden the waves start surging, roaring and unstoppable...that's just the way it is, it's not up to you anymore, you've just got to roll with it. And then the wind stops and the waves die down and what's left is that vast expanse once more, all worn out, the crashing waves mere memory."[49]

MARGARET CAVENDISH

woman finds herself stranded at the North Pole and wanders through an interdimensional gateway, where she is greeted by alien creatures and crowned their empress. Her new planet, home to bizarre technology and fantastical, wind-powered vehicles, is called *The Blazing World*. It sounds like a typical science fiction novel, with one crucial difference: it was written in 1666. Its author was the Duchess of Newcastle-upon-Tyne Margaret Cavendish (1623–1673) – a woman considered so eccentric that she became known as "Mad Madge" and is now hailed as the author of one of the earliest science fiction books in existence.

In her prologue to *The Blazing World*, Margaret writes: "That though I cannot be Henry the Fifth, or Charles the Second; yet, I will endeavour to be, Margaret the First: and, though I have neither Power, Time nor Occasion, to be a great Conqueror, like Alexander, or Caesar; yet, rather than not be Mistress of a World, since Fortune and the Fates would give me none, I have made One of my own."[50] It's a sentiment that many a sci-fi fan will appreciate: if the real world lets you down, why not escape via speculative fiction?

Margaret, however, was not the shy or retiring kind. In her day, she hobnobbed with and held her own against philosophers like Thomas Hobbes, René Descartes and Henry More. She was the first woman to receive a formal invite to the Royal Society, which would later shut its doors to women until 1945; she scandalized England when she appeared topless, her nipples tinted red, in her husband's play; she was mobbed by people in Hyde Park. Little wonder that the diarist Samuel Pepys once said of her: "The whole story of this lady is a romance, and all she do is romantick."[51]

Born in 1623 to wealthy but untitled parents, Margaret sought her independence when she became maid of honour to Henrietta Maria, the Catholic wife of the doomed King Charles I. Charles's execution sent his widow fleeing to France, and Margaret dutifully followed. In Paris, she met her husband-to-be, William Cavendish (who was then the Marquess of Newcastle-upon-Tyne and became the 1st Duke 20 years after their marriage). William was three decades her senior, but very much Margaret's intellectual equal. It was William, a keen amateur scholar, who introduced her to pre-eminent natural philosophers, opening up a new world of scientific knowledge to Margaret.

With William's support, Margaret was able to publish her own work, which included everything from philosophical treatises to plays and poetry. At a time when most female authors wrote anonymously, Margaret published under her own name. She also had her portrait engraved on the frontispiece of her volumes, just to make doubly sure people knew who had written it.

The scandal that accompanied Margaret, however, was sometimes enough to drown her work. Her debut volume of poetry, *Poems and*

Fancies – the first such work published by a woman under her own name – led one aristocrat to remark: "There are many soberer people in Bedlam."[52] Others suspected that she hadn't even written her books at all, which only caused Margaret to double down on her larger-than-life public persona. She began wearing men's clothing in an attempt to fit in with the masculine scientific and literary establishment.

All this served to cement her ridiculousness in the eyes of English society, though it didn't stop people from chasing her carriage through the streets to catch a glimpse of her. "There is as much expectation of her coming to Court, that so people may come to see her, as if it were the Queen of Sheba,"[53] sniffed Pepys – though he queued up with the rest of the hoi polloi to watch her step through the doors of the Royal Society.

Margaret did not discriminate between genre or literary form – all were up for grabs and open to debate. Take *The Blazing World*, which can be read as a proto-feminist text in which women rule supreme, and also as a satire on the scientific method, with its "lice-men"[54] who futilely "endeavoured to measure all things to a hairs-breadth, and weigh them to an Atom"[55]. It wasn't just her writing that was ahead of its time. In an age when most men subscribed to materialism and mechanistic philosophy, Margaret argued vociferously that everything in the universe was made of corporeal matter – and in a period when vivisection was the norm, she argued for animal rights.

Despite the cries that she was mad or deranged, Margaret knew she had a place in history – she was just unfortunate enough to have been born several steps ahead of everyone else. Not that it put her off literature. As she wrote in her autobiography, "I verily believe some censuring Readers will scornfully say, 'Why hath this Lady writ her own life?...' I answer that it is true that 'tis of no purpose to the Reader, but it is to the Authoress. I write it for my own sake not theirs."[6]

HERMYNIA ZUR MÜHLEN

ermynia Zur Mühlen (1883–1951) was many things: an Austrian heiress with avowed socialist politics, a committed anti-fascist who escaped the Nazis and an author who published everything from detective novels to left-wing fairy tales. Everything you need to know about Hermynia, however, can be summed up by the Anchor Society, the self-described "society for the improvement of the world",[57] which she founded at the tender age of 13. Its membership mainly consisted of Hermynia's cousins, three girls from her town and her British grandmother, Countess Isabella Luisa von Wydenbruck, but it nevertheless signalled something of Hermynia's ambitions – she wanted to do nothing less than change the world. The first aim of the Anchor Society? Abolish the nobility.

This may sound contradictory – self-defeating, even – for someone born into one of Vienna's most distinguished families. But Hermynia's nickname wasn't the Red Countess for nothing – her socialist tendencies were nurtured from childhood and ran deep in her blood. Hermynia's upbringing was left to her relatively progressive grandma, with her equally liberal uncle dropping in to answer any questions of political philosophy posed by his precocious niece. She was encouraged by both to read widely, think deeply and, above all, care intensely about social injustice.

"I had aspired at one time to be a circus rider or the female leader of a noble robber band, but from now on I recognized only two really superior callings: that of member of the House of Delegates or that of journalist,"[58] she wrote of her early teenage years. But Hermynia soon realized that her views were significantly more radical than her family's. When she proudly read out a column calling for the corrupt Austrian government to be hanged, her uncle turned to her grandmother and said, sorrowfully, "The child will end up on the gallows herself one day."[59]

Hermynia's politics solidified further over the course of a brief marriage to a dour Baltic nobleman, who owned an estate in Estonia. Their unhappy union proved useful as a crash course in the cruelty of landowners to their workers. "I had become a 'class enemy',"[60] Hermynia wryly observed in her memoirs. In 1913, she fell ill and was prescribed treatment at a sanatorium in Davos, Switzerland, where she met the Jewish translator Stefan Isidore Klein, the man who would become her second husband.

Over the next three decades, Hermynia translated over 70 Russian, English and French novels into German. Not content with translating other people's words, she began writing books of her own – first a detective series under the pen name Lawrence H Desberry, with Hermynia cheekily identifying herself as the translator; then a collection of subversive fairy tales that aimed to introduce socialist ideas to children and was translated into no less than nine languages, including Chinese; two coming-of-age novels that discussed taboo subjects like abortion and menstruation with unusual frankness; and countless columns and sketches for left-wing newspapers. She was soon regarded as "one of the best known women writers of the Weimar Republic".[61]

By this time, Hermynia and Stefan were living in Frankfurt and found themselves under police surveillance thanks to their Communist leanings. Hermynia was even briefly accused of high treason (the charge was later dropped). After Hitler became Chancellor in 1933, however, they decided to flee for Austria, where Hermynia was enraged by her former homeland's apathy to the rise of the Nazis. She produced her boldest work yet, *Unsere Töchter die Nazinen* ("Our Daughters the Nazis"), about three women whose daughters are brainwashed by National Socialism. It was two years before a publisher in Austria took it on, only for it to be banned immediately.

In the midst of this drama, Hermynia and Stefan found themselves in dire financial straits. Although the Red Countess had long since renounced her titles, she had inherited some money from her mother's estate. But there was one crucial caveat: she had to sign documents confirming that she was of Aryan heritage. She refused to put her name on the dotted line, choosing solidarity with the Jewish people – and her husband – over financial salvation.

In 1938, Austria was annexed and the couple sought refuge in Slovakia, where the long arm of Nazi Germany reached them once again as the newly declared Slovak Republic was occupied by Hitler. For the fourth and final time, they decided to flee – this time to Britain, where they lived a penniless life in a suburban town in Hertfordshire. Hermynia's health suffered in the damp English climate, and she died without finishing her last novel. She was a long way from Austria, and even farther from the privileged little girl who had cycled through town shouting, "Down with the nobility!"[62]

But this was, perhaps, Hermynia's intention all along. She wrote in her memoirs: "I broke with my old world and dared to leap into the new. I learned to work, to stand on my own two feet. I was no longer a single individual struggling senselessly against overpowering opponents, but a tiny part of a great whole which I could serve, in however modest measure, to the best of my ability."[63]

FRAÇOISE DE GRAFFIGNY

rançoise de Graffigny (1695–1758) was once Europe's best-known female author, but went through hell and back to get there. Born in Nancy, France, somewhere in the middling ranks of the *petite noblesse*, she married an officer to the Duke of Lorraine in 1712, before she had even turned 17. The marriage was doomed from the start – her husband, François Huguet, was a gambling addict and a violent drunk, and he took out his anger on his wife.

In another example of what Françoise frequently bemoaned as her *guignon* ("ill luck"), all three of their children died young and within a few years of each other. Françoise's husband was later hauled to jail on charges of domestic violence; she obtained a legal separation and was summarily ejected into the ranks of the newly divorced. He died two years later, after frittering away most of Françoise's dowry. Her parents made it abundantly clear that their now destitute daughter was on her own.

The newly widowed Françoise was poor but abundantly charming, and she managed to inveigle her way into the court of Lorraine in Lunéville, where she served the dowager duchess and regent, Élisabeth Charlotte d'Orléans. Here, she began to write for the first time – mostly plays written with poets like François-Antoine Devaux (or "Panpan", as she nicknamed him), who would later become her closest confidant. It was at Lunéville that she also met Léopold Desmarest, a handsome young cavalry officer who was 13 years her junior. They promptly struck up a passionate love affair, which would last well into her forties. However, Françoise's *guignon* struck again when the duchy of Lorraine was ceded to France and its court dissolved, leaving her back where she started.

Salvation came in the unlikely form of Voltaire, the polymath author and philosopher, who had visited Lunéville; he invited Françoise to join him and the equally brilliant scientist Émilie du Châtelet at the château they shared in Cirey, France. But Françoise's three months at Cirey came to an unlucky end when Émilie accused her of illicitly transcribing a copy of Voltaire's poem *La Pucelle d'Orléans* ("The Maid of Orleans"), forcing their now unwelcome guest to flee to Paris.

Françoise, penniless in Paris, was forced to hop between convent lodgings and her friends' homes. Even more disastrous was her relationship with Léopold, which came to an end when he dramatically left her for another woman after rinsing Françoise of whatever money she had left. But the adaptable author-in-exile quickly found her feet in her new city. Her friendship with the celebrated actress Jeanne Quinault introduced her to some of the most exciting poets and writers in Paris, and Françoise found herself newly inspired at Jeanne's raucous dinner salon, known to all as Société du Bout-du-Banc.

In 1747, Françoise published *Letters from a Peruvian Woman*, her first book. The epistolary novel tells of Zilia, an Incan princess who is abducted by Spanish conquistadors from the Temple of the Sun in Peru and rescued by French sailors while en route to Europe as the spoils of war. As she steps into French society, Zilia comes to realize that her life as a cloistered temple virgin was not so different from the lives of women in her new country, and that in both places the women are consistently underestimated and demeaned by the men around them. Instead, Zilia chooses to spurn men for a life of solitude and study.

Letters from a Peruvian Woman was a sensation – within a year of publication, the printers had issued 14 editions. She quickly followed it with the script for the domestic comedy *Cénie*, a triumph at the Comédie-Française. Now the biggest names in literature and politics swarmed to her home near the leafy walkways of the Jardin du Luxembourg, and she played host to everyone from Rousseau to Montesquieu. Though Françoise enjoyed the "the pleasure of living with people of wit, good sense, and reason", she found her new-found success sometimes exasperating: "It is horribly fatiguing to talk all day just to say nothing."[64]

Through it all, she continued to exchange letters with her loyal Panpan. Three centuries on, it is her correspondence – amounting to some 7,000 pages – that is now seen as her true masterpiece. Françoise might have told François-Antoine, "I have no interest in getting mixed up in the affairs of great people: I could not withhold my reflections, they would be a bit too philosophical,"[65] but her letters say otherwise. They reveal not just her innermost thoughts, but a historically significant and startlingly vivid portrait of 18th-century French society in all its high drama. "From 1750 to 1758…she was the foremost woman of letters in France, if not in Europe, and she counted the most distinguished writers, government officials, and foreign visitors among the guests at her salon,"[66] notes historian English Showalter.

Shortly after premiering her second play, *Aristides' Daughter*, which was badly received and dented her reputation, Françoise died of a seizure. Until this century, when her correspondence was unearthed at an auction in 1960s New York, she had largely dwelled in obscurity. Françoise would have been astonished at the reversal of her fortunes. In all probability, however, she would have been delighted whatever happened. "I will live today," she once wrote gratefully, "and that is a lot, to have another day."[67]

KĀTERINA TE HEIKŌKŌ MATAIRA

here are close to seven thousand languages spoken around the world, but scientists believe that up to a quarter of them are threatened or close to extinction. By the mid-20th century, the Māori language (or *te reo* Māori, as it is known in New Zealand) was close to becoming one of them. Until, that is, Kāterina Te Heikōkō Mataira (1932–2011) got involved.

Born in picturesque Tokomaru Bay on the North Island of New Zealand in 1932, the author, educator and passionate grassroots leader grew up speaking her native tongue and saw the value in preserving the centuries-old language. She faced an uphill battle. Though Māori was spoken widely in the 1800s, even by *pākehā* (European) settlers in the country, it had entered a decades-long decline by the 20th century. One older Māori tribal leader, Sir James Hēnare, even recalled being beaten for speaking it in school grounds. "If you want to earn your bread and butter," he was told, "you must speak English."[26]

His teachers may have been misguided, but they weren't wrong. English, the lingua franca of the increasingly dominant *pākehā* colonists, had become the language of commerce and education. Even though *pākehā* lingo borrowed Māori words like "kiwi" and "taboo" (*tapu*), the Māori language struggled to adapt in the same way. By the 1980s, less than 20 percent of Māori could be classed as native speakers of their indigenous language.

Kāterina had originally trained as a teacher, and in 1973 she learned of a pedagogical method known as the Silent Way. She was studying in Fiji at the time and was amazed at how quickly Peace Corps volunteers on the island had picked up the local language. It was the result of a ten-week crash course organized along Silent Way lines, in which teachers are trained to instruct students in the target language only, guiding them to proficiency by using visual cues in the form of coloured rods to represent sentence structure and grammar.

She brought the teaching method back to New Zealand and, with fellow educator Ngoi Pēwhairangi, set about adapting the Silent Way as a means to resuscitate their dying language. The resulting Te Ataarangi teaching programme – and the Kura Kaupapa Māori language immersion schools that she founded – helped to reverse decades of decline. Sweeping across New Zealand, they reintroduced Māori children and adults to their long-forgotten native tongue.

There were tweaks, of course. The Silent Way was created by Egyptian mathematician-turned-educator Caleb Gattegno, and Kāterina's genius was to adapt it to Māori custom and tradition. Te Ataarangi instructors stressed the value of *ngākau māhaki* – humility and respect – to their students. English was banned entirely in the classroom, and learners were encouraged to listen attentively to others and not to interrupt.

"[I would] turn up at the *marae* (meeting ground), me with my pencil and paper," New Zealand politician and Māori Party co-founder Tariana Turia remembered in a tribute to Kāterina."They would promptly tell me to put away my *'pākehā* brain' – it was all *'Whakarongo* (listen)! *Titiro* (look)! *Kōrero* (speak)!'"[27] Bit by bit, Kāterina's beloved language began making a comeback.

Of course, Kāterina knew that schools weren't enough to assure its survival. As a child, she didn't have many books growing up, but she devoured the Children's Corner pages in her mother's English copies of the magazine *Woman's Weekly* and adored storytime with her father. "My father was a brilliant storyteller," she said. "Many of his stories were about his own life. They were full of real people and real events. There were scary ones too. He loved to tell ghost stories, then send one of us kids outside to fetch wood for the fire."[28]

Sometime in the 1970s, the New Zealand Department of Education invited Kāterina to a combative panel discussion on Māori literature. When a *pākehā* audience member confronted her on the value of publishing anything in a "stone-age language that was incapable of expressing modern ideas and concepts",[29] she was incensed enough to take him up on his challenge. Kāterina showed its place in the future by writing a book in the most forward-thinking genre on the planet: science fiction.

In 1975, she became one of the first women to publish in Māori with *Te Ātea*, a visionary science fiction novel that followed a group of survivors as they take to the stars after a nuclear holocaust. Kāterina had to invent new words to contain her universe, including *waka-ātea* for spaceship and *pikopoto wā* for warp time. *"Te Ātea* was revolutionary when it appeared in 1975 – sophisticated science fiction expressed in *te reo* Māori and complemented by the artwork of Para Matchitt,"[30] remembered Pita Sharples, the former New Zealand Minister for Māori Development. Two more books followed, including a sequel to her debut work, along with a string of award-winning children's books, all written in the language that she had done so much to preserve.

At the age of 79, she was appointed as a Dame in the Queen's Birthday Honours List in recognition of her contributions to Māori culture. But perhaps the greatest compliment to her work came from the Rapa Nui people of Easter Island, who invited her to their home to help stave off the death of their language – by developing their own version of Te Ataarangi.

 always wanted to write," Neshani Andreas (1964–2011) told *Sister Namibia* magazine. "I wrote as a child, in high school, as long as I can remember."[68]

Namibia was not yet a country when Neshani Andreas was born. She grew up as the second of eight children in what was then known as South West Africa, a former German colony controlled by South Africa – a control that extended to introducing apartheid. In the years that followed, the Namibian people led an armed uprising against their South African rulers, resulting in the deaths of up to 25,000 people during the 24 years of war.

Over these years of upheaval, Neshani – a shy, dreamy girl – cultivated ambitions that would take her far away from the port town of Walvis Bay, where her parents worked in the local fish factory. She never told anyone about her dream of being an author. In the harsh climes of pre-independence Namibia, being a writer was not encouraged. In fact, it was pretty much unheard of. Instead, Neshani kept her writing to herself and retreated into her imagination. "I lived in a world that did not make sense to anybody else," she said. "On the other hand I had to fit into a world around me that did not make much sense to me."[69]

Even after Neshani trained as a teacher and travelled to the north to work in rural Namibia, she kept filling page after page with notes, keeping them close to her for safekeeping. "I wrote as a schoolgirl, in high school…and I continued to write for myself, just pages of this and that, they became part of my luggage when moving from one place to the next, they were my most treasured things."[70]

Neshani moved to Namibia's capital Windhoek for a postgraduate degree in education aged 32, and became an associate director for the American Peace Corps. Namibia was a fledgling country, still finding its feet after years of war. Then came a chance encounter with a Peace Corps volunteer, Reed Dickson, who not only supported her writing but read it to boot. Neshani had shared her writing with friends before with unspectacular results – nobody took her seriously. But Reed was different – he wanted to see her work the instant she mentioned it. "This was one of the most treasured moments in my life," she said. "I had met the first person in my life who showed interest and understanding in my writing."[71]

It was the only encouragement Neshani needed. She bought a laptop and set to work on a novel that was to become *The Purple Violet of Oshaantu*, a tale of two village women in the north, Mee Ali and Kauna, whose marriages diverge in happiness and tragedy – Mee Ali is blessed with a good marriage, while Kauna is abused and cheated on by her husband. In her clear and direct language, Neshani covered everything from the AIDS crisis to local superstition and domestic violence. It is also the story of enduring female friendship in the face of abominable violence. Mee Ali recalls witnessing Kauna's husband beating her: "I will remember this sight of Kauna for as long as I live. Blood mixed with sand all over her face, in her mouth, nose, eyes, ears, head and clothes, and the sight of her children crying helplessly."[72]

The book was based on Neshani's own experience of rural life while teaching in the countryside, and she wanted to do justice to the lives of ordinary Namibians – to document the daily activities that make up everyday life, from "travelling in overcrowded minibuses"[73] to "selling and buying at markets".[74]

In that sense, she was an anomaly among other Namibian writers, who were concerned with the historical battles of the past and the country's future as a nation. "People were still talking about the struggle, about exile and returning home," she remembered. "Writers were expected to write about great events, to glorify the past and the present, to glorify people."[75]

In 2001, *The Purple Violet of Oshaantu* became the first Namibian novel to be published overseas as part of the Heinemann African Writers Series. But success did not spell recognition – at least not in her country. Some questioned whether she had written the book by herself, or assumed that everything that had occurred in the book had actually happened to her. "Why do you write something like this? Are you up to something?"[76] asked a few others.

"Writing is still not encouraged by Namibian society," she explained. "It is not regarded as a respectable job, as something that has any benefit."[77] But Neshani kept writing, just as she had all those decades before she published her book. When she died of lung cancer in 2011, she had only just completed the manuscript for her second book.

It has yet to be published.

RADCLYFFE HALL

he year was 1928, and Radclyffe Hall (1880–1943) was sitting in a courthouse on Bow Street, London, watching as her novel *The Well of Loneliness* was sentenced to its doom. "The publication of this book," Magistrate Sir Chartres Biron declared, "is an offence against public decency, an obscene libel, and I shall order it to be destroyed."[78] All copies of the book were seized and burned.

What was the crime that had been committed? Radclyffe's novel, which the then Home Secretary branded "inherently obscene and gravely detrimental to the public interest,"[79] promoted that most unsaintly of sins: homosexuality. Radclyffe, who described herself as a "congenital invert",[80] had, in fact, set out to write it as a radical plea for understanding on behalf of women who loved women, aimed squarely at the "frequently cruel and nearly always thoughtless and ignorant world".[81]

"No one was better qualified to write the subject in fiction than an experienced novelist like myself," she wrote in a letter to a friend, "who was actually one of the people about whom she was writing and was thus in a position to understand their spiritual, mental and physical reactions, their joys and their sorrows..."[82]

She was rewarded with public disgust instead. But Radclyffe (or "John", as she was known to her friends) was used to rejection. Her father, Radclyffe Radclyffe-Hall, was an inveterate cad and a wife beater. Radclyffe was only a month old when her father ditched her and her mother, Mary Jane Hall. Her mother got married again, to Albert Visetti, a half-Italian singer and opera tutor, who repaid her mother by making advances on Radclyffe, when she was only ten years old.

It came as a blessed relief when Radclyffe turned 21 and inherited her father's estate, along with her financial freedom – especially after her mother discovered her passionate affair with Visetti's protégée, a voluptuous soprano named Agnes Nicholls. Radclyffe embarked on a new life of finely tailored suits, luxury and romance, wooing women with the wealth at her disposal. She was "free to make my own life, free to go where I please", buying a country house, dogs and expensive horses, and she began writing verse after a "hard day's hunting".[83]

In 1907, Radclyffe met Mabel Batten, a well-travelled socialite and wife to a high-ranking colonial officer in India. "She was to become a spur to my work and from the first my true unfailing inspiration,"[84] Radclyffe wrote.

Mabel was the one who first encouraged her writing, though it took a few decades for Radclyffe to find her feet as a novelist. In 1926, she found success with *Adam's Breed*, which followed the spiritual travails of a down-on-his-luck waiter. It sold close to 30,000 copies in three weeks, winning the prestigious Prix Femina and the James Tait Black Prize. By this time, however, Mabel had been replaced in Radclyffe's affections by Una Troubridge, Mabel's 28-year-old cousin. Radclyffe would remain with Una for the rest of her life.

With her predilection for the finer things in life and her enormous fortune, Radclyffe was, in many ways, an upper-class toff and a small "c" conservative at heart. (For example, when she heard of suffragettes smashing windows in London, she denounced them in a letter to the *Pall Mall Gazette*.)

She was, however, a pioneer when it came to LGBTQI rights. Just a few months before the publication of Virginia Woolf's *Orlando*, Radclyffe launched *The Well of Loneliness* into the world. To some extent, she knew of the storm that would greet its debut. "I have put my pen at the service of some of the most persecuted and misunderstood people in the world," she wrote to her publisher in 1928. "So far as I know nothing of the kind has ever been attempted before in fiction."

The coming-of-age novel follows Stephen Gordon, a misunderstood but noble heroine who struggles with her sexuality but ultimately issues a cry for equality on behalf of all "inverts". "Acknowledge us, oh God, before the whole world," Stephen declares toward the end of the book. "Give us also the right to our existence!"[85]

When the trial came, Radclyffe's publisher sent out more than a hundred letters to literary supporters he hoped would vouch for *The Well of Loneliness* in court. Many declined, or gave half-hearted excuses that Virginia Woolf herself sniffily described as "the weak of heart father, or a cousin who is about to have twins".[86] Radclyffe was exhausted by the time the trial was over; her next three novels did not attract the same notoriety.

She died believing that *The Well of Loneliness* would never be read, and that her attempt at truth-telling was as good as dust. Nothing could be farther from the truth. Eighteen years after Radclyffe died of cancer, Una wrote in a biography of her great love:

"What nobody foresaw was that the re-publication in Paris would be followed by translation into eleven languages, by the triumph of the book in the United States of America and the sale of more than a million copies. The author herself would probably have felt less tired had she been able to look ahead, to read in advance some of the many thousands of letters that came to her later from men and women in every walk of life, of every age and every nationality in all parts of the world, and that continued to reach her through the years and come now, even after her death, from remote places where that death is still unknown."[87]

Historians,
Academics
&
Diarists

ESTHER HILLESUM

esterbork transit camp in the Netherlands – the last stop for thousands of Jews en route to concentration camps – is known for hosting Anne Frank before she was taken to Bergen-Belsen. But this place of misery was briefly home to another Dutch memoirist, whose diary was also published posthumously: Esther "Etty" Hillesum (1914–1943), a young student whose deeply candid and spiritually profound record of life under Nazi occupation languished unpublished for decades.

Born in 1914 in Middelburg, Netherlands, Etty began her journal in 1941. She had escaped an unstable home life to seek a new one as a Russian language student at the University of Amsterdam, but was having trouble adjusting in her new city. Amsterdam had already lived under German occupation for a year, and as the new trend of psychoanalysis swept Europe, Etty sought the help of Julius Spier, a charismatic Jung-influenced therapist who believed in palmistry and literally wrestled with patients in order to shake off their demons.

It may sound like quackery now, but Etty clearly found something valuable in it. Julius introduced her to the Bible and the writings of Rainer Maria Rilke and St Augustine, and she would draw on them as a source of mystic revelation and comfort in the years to come. Etty and Julius eventually became lovers, and she came to regard him as someone who had sparked her spiritual awakening – Julius was, as she put it, "the one who had attended at the birth of my soul".[1]

Etty had not been raised to be particularly Jewish (her family had scarcely gone to synagogue), but she began thinking deeply on the nature of belief and God. One day, she found herself unexpectedly sinking to her knees on her bathroom mat in prayer. "There is a really deep well inside me," she muses. "And in it dwells God. Sometimes I am there, too. But more often stones and grit block the well, and God is buried beneath. Then He must be dug out again."[2]

Taken on its own, her diary would be a remarkable chronicle of one young woman's journey toward faith. But as the Holocaust began to

ensnare Jewish people in Amsterdam, Etty found herself recording the fate of her people, too. She knew what was happening; she had heard the rumours of the gas chambers to the east. "What is at stake is our impending destruction and annihilation; we can have no more illusions about that," she wrote tersely. "They are out to destroy us completely, we must accept that and go on from there."[3]

In the face of overwhelming cruelty, however, she retained her compassion: "Nazi barbarism evokes the same kind of barbarism in ourselves," she wrote. "We have to reject that barbarism within us, we must not fan the hatred within us, because if we do, the world will not be able to pull itself one inch further out of the mire."[4]

Knowing that she herself might be called up for internment at any point, Etty instead volunteered at Westerbork, administering aid and succour to the ill and elderly as they lay in wait for the concentration camps. She called herself the "ears and eyes of a piece of Jewish history"[5] to "wield this slender fountain pen as if it were a hammer, and my words will have to be so many hammer strokes with which to beat out the story of our fate".[6]

Etty grew resolute in her desire to remain at Westerbork and share the destiny of her people. At a time when thousands of Jews went into hiding to escape the gas chamber, she even fought off a friend who attempted to kidnap her to safety. "Those two months behind barbed wire have been the two richest and most intense months of my life, in which my highest values were so deeply confirmed,"[7] she wrote. In the summer of 1943, she passed her diary to a friend in the hope that it would be published. It was finally published in 1981, entitled *An Interrupted Life*, and was immediately hailed as a testament to hope and faith in the face of unimaginable tragedy. Shortly before she was sent to Auschwitz with her family, Etty wrote of Westerbork:

The misery here is quite terrible, and yet, late at night when the day has slunk away into the depths behind me, I often walk with a spring in my step along the barbed wire. And then, time and again, it soars straight from my heart – I can't help it, that's just the way it is, like some elementary force – the feeling that life is glorious and magnificent, and that one day we shall be building a whole new world.[8]

ANNA KOMNENE

t's often said that history is written by the victors, but, as literary critic Barbara Newman points out, it is just as accurate to say that history also tends to be "written by men, for men, about men".[9] That's where Byzantine princess Anna Komnene (1083–1153) comes in. In her old age, Anna took on the daunting task of documenting the reign of her deceased father, Emperor Alexios Komnenos, "the shining light of the world".[10] Today, her *Alexiad* remains a primary source for much of what we know about the dramas and delights of 12th-century Constantinople, and Anna its number one historian.

Anna was the eldest of Alexios's seven children, born in Constantinople at the heart of Byzantine power and with both the constitution and the intelligence to match. Her mother, Empress Irene Doukaina, instilled in her a love of books and learning; in the *Alexiad*, Anna compares her to the Greek goddess of wisdom Athena. In one passage, Anna complains that people in Constantinople would rather play draughts (checkers) than study poetry and history. "It grieves me to see the total neglect of general education," she wrote. "It makes my blood boil, for I myself spent much time on these same exercises."[11]

Alexios gently pushed her toward penning elegies and the like, but Anna's impulse toward hard-headed historical writing won out – and there was nobody she thought more deserving of posterity than her dad. "I approach the task with no intention of flaunting my skill as a writer," she wrote. "My concern is rather that a career so brilliant should not go unrecorded in the future, since even the greatest exploits, unless by some chance their memory is preserved and guarded in history, vanish in silent darkness."[12]

Anna viewed her father through rose-tinted glasses, but she was also a born historian. Anticipating accusations of bias, she scoured the palace archives and interviewed eyewitnesses from her father's many military battles. "History must by its very nature be founded on truth,"[13] she explained.

She had one advantage over other historians, too – she had lived through the very events she recounted, and she didn't shy away from recording them down to the last detail. Anna described her own father's death with the same attention that she lavished on the inner machinations of the imperial court and the mighty fleets of triremes (ancient warships powered by oars as well as sails) setting off for war. As her father lay dying, Anna even recorded private conversations in the royal bedchamber: "It's like a dead-weight of stone lying on my heart and cutting short my breathing," the ailing emperor told his wife. "I can't understand the reason for it, nor why such pain afflicts me."[14]

But the *Alexiad* is no dry historical chronicle. In Anna's many charming asides and digressions, you can snatch a glimpse of the woman behind the weighty book – sweetly devoted to her family. When narrating her father's death, she suddenly draws back the curtain and speaks frankly of her grief: "Even now I cannot believe that I am still alive and writing this account of the emperor's death. I put my hands to my eyes, wondering if what I am relating here is not all a dream – or maybe it is not a dream: perhaps it is a delusion and I am mad, the victim of some extraordinary and monstrous hallucination...Why did I not surrender my soul too and die with him?"[15]

Eventually, the *Alexiad* stretched to 15 volumes, including one dedicated to the First Crusade, the only extant Byzantine record of the vicious and protracted battle that would go on to redefine the Middle Ages. Anna's story proves just as complicated – successive historians have attacked her as a power-hungry pretender to the throne; the Byzantine answer to Lady Macbeth.

Five decades after her death, historian Niketas Choniates claimed that she and her mother conspired to depose Anna's brother John and install her husband, Nikephoros Bryennios, as emperor. There was little direct evidence of this failed coup, but it didn't stop Choniates from speculating on Nikephoros's punishment when the plot collapsed: "It is said that Kaisarissa Anna, disgusted with her husband's frivolous behaviour and distraught in her anger, and being a shrew by nature, felt justified in strongly contracting her vagina when Bryennios' penis entered deep inside her, thus causing him great pain."[16]

Factually speaking, it is highly unlikely that a woman is capable of squeezing *quite* so powerfully, but this account set the tone for centuries to come. In 1901, French historian Charles Diehl cast Anna in the role of the "proud princess":[17] "She considered the throne legitimately and essentially hers, she thought herself so superior to her detested younger brother."[18]

As historian Leonora Neville points out, Diehl and his predecessors failed to include any proof of the elaborate plot that would have allowed Anna to take the throne by proxy; instead, she is assumed to be a schemer because, well, that's just what clever women are. It is only now that contemporary scholars are beginning to uncover the real Anna Komnene – a woman who, literally, wrote herself into the history books.

MARIE VASSILTCHIKOV

he Berlin Diaries 1940–45, Marie "Missie" Vassiltchikov's (1917–1978) memoir of World War II-era Europe, is a study in contrasts – it begins with Marie's breathless recollection of a fabulous ball at a foreign embassy in Berlin and ends with her daring escape from the Red Army in bombed-out Vienna.

Marie had already lived through one world-changing event: the Bolshevik Revolution of 1917. The Russian princess was born on the wrong side of the peasant uprising; her aristocratic family were forced to give up their land and had been on the run ever since. By the time she ended up in Berlin, her parents had burned through all their cash.

Luckily, Marie knew four languages and had a wealth of social capital to fall back on, even in a wartime city besieged by instability. In her clear-sighted, matter-of-fact prose, Marie documents a surreal vision of aristocrats going about a nightmarish daily business – oysters and champagne at the Eden Hotel and 2am parties at the Grunewald, followed by stays in a bomb shelter and the terror and confusion of nightly Allied raids. "We tried to avoid standing under what we thought were houses," Marie writes of hiding in a public bunker, "preferring the open streets, where nothing could crash down on top of us except the bombs themselves."[19]

After a job at the American Embassy fell through and strapped for cash, Marie ended up working as an assistant at the German Foreign Office. It turned out to be a hotbed for the German Resistance; her boss, Adam von Trott, was one of the leaders of Operation Valkyrie, the July 1944 plot to kill Hitler. "It is all very hush-hush, but Loremarie [a friend and Foreign Office co-worker], who has also moved

out to Potsdam, keeps me informed about what I call 'the Conspiracy',"[20] Marie wrote.

On her part, Marie claimed to remain an innocent observer, though she despised the Nazis as much as her friends did. A week before the launch of Operation Valkyrie, Adam trusted her enough to let her in on the details of the plot: "We don't see eye to eye on this because I continue to find that too much time is being lost perfecting the details, whereas to me only one thing is really important now – the physical elimination of the man," she wrote. "What happens to Germany once he is dead can be seen to later."[21]

Hitler survived the assassination attempt, and Adam was among the 7,000 suspected conspirators subsequently rounded up by the Gestapo. He was executed at Plötzensee Prison less than ten days later. Several of Marie's friends chose suicide over torture, or slipped out of the country entirely. Marie and Loremarie charmed their way past the prison guards, bravely hoping to pass care packages and food to their incarcerated friends. Marie even thought of going to Joseph Goebbels to beg mercy for Adam, but was convinced out of it by a friend. Hitler's notorious Minister of Propaganda, she was told, "is a real sewer rat, and that if I caught his notice in the slightest way, I would drag the whole family into it."[22] She decided against it.

And anyway, it was far too late. Many of Marie's comrades-in-arms had already been executed on charges of treason. In the safety of a Russian Orthodox priest's apartment, Marie held a memorial service for the dead and prayed for those still left alive. "I was the only person present," she remembered, "and I cried throughout it horribly."[23]

As the noose tightened around her circle, Marie left Berlin to work as a nurse in Vienna. But Austria was no refuge, either – she arrived just in time for Allied bombs to leave a fifth of the city in rubble. "Today's raid was particularly bad," she wrote. "The debris of a shot-down American plane was scattered all over the pavement in front of [Liechtenstein Palace]; it was still burning merrily and now and then there were little explosions – the ammunition going off. Nearly all the crew had perished. Only one of them bailed out but got stuck on a roof gable, which tore off both his legs."[24] There were so many dead that Vienna ran out of coffins. Marie managed to make it out to the Austrian Alps in time for US troops to liberate the region, and she married a US army captain shortly after.

Her diary was published posthumously – a testament to the on-the-ground ravages of war, seen through the eyes of a very unlikely source.

Sometime around the year 1000 – about the same time that Murasaki Shikibu (*see* page 70) was writing *The Tale of Genji* – Sei Shōnagon (*c.*966–*c.*1017/25) was creating a very different literary work in the Japanese imperial court. It is now known as *The Pillow Book*, and its would-be author had modest aims: "I merely wrote for my personal amusement things that I myself have thought and felt, and I never intended that it should be placed alongside other books and judged on a par with them."[25]

Murasaki, her fellow lady-in-waiting, sniffed that her rival was "dreadfully conceited",[26] adding that "people who have become so precious that they go out of their way to try and be sensitive in the most unpromising situations, trying to capture every moment of interest, however slight, are bound to look ridiculous and superficial."[27] True, *The Pillow Book* is a very different beast to *The Tale of Genji*. The work has been described as a pastiche, and it certainly is something of a delightful mess, with intimate diary entries and memories of courtly life veering off into charming lists of her likes and dislikes and opinions.

But it was in attempting to capture every fleeting detail of her era – from her stylish gentlemen callers right down to her everyday annoyances – that Sei Shōnagon hit on something true and eternal. It's easy to feel like Heian-era Japan is not so far away from our century's own social foibles when Sei is tartly describing her list of "infuriating things",[28] such as "a guest who arrives when you have something urgent to do, and stays talking for ages" or "someone who butts in when you're talking and smugly provides the ending herself", or when she recounts the dispiriting nature of "those times when you send someone a poem you're rather pleased with, and fail to receive one in reply".[29] (Ghosting, anyone?)

We know very little of Sei's background. "Shōnagon" denotes the rank of junior councillor, while Sei is short for her family name of Kiyohara. As the daughter of a minor governor, Sei was already in her late twenties when she was yanked from the provinces to serve the Empress Teishi in 993, and she was a devoted lady-in-waiting up until the death of her mistress in childbirth in 1000. After that, there is precious little trace of Sei in official records. She was once married, but we do not know the name of her husband. She took several lovers at court, and *The Pillow Book* records her judgment on their hopeless bumbling: "I do wish men, when they're taking their leave from a lady at dawn, wouldn't insist on adjusting their clothes to a nicety, or fussily tying their lacquered cap securely into place," she sighed. "One does want a lover's dawn departure to be tasteful."[30]

Sei also claimed that she began *The Pillow Book* by a sheer accident of fate. A palace minister had presented her Empress with a rare bundle of spare paper, which was in turn gifted to her. "I set to work with this boundless pile of paper to fill it to the last sheet with all manner of odd things, so no doubt there's much in these pages that makes no sense," Sei wrote. Her diary came to light when she accidentally left it out on a mat, only for a visitor to circulate it around the court. The scholar and translator Meredith McKinney has pointed out, however, there there is a "strong whiff of false humility in these disclaimers".[31] It is unlikely that Sei would have left out something so precious without knowing what she was doing.

All great Japanese literature at the time was written in kanji, the formal script based on Chinese. It was kanji that was used for all official state records, and it was solely deployed by men. Women used the Japanese script of hiragana, which was only thought appropriate for poetry and was even sneeringly referred to as *onnadé* ("the women's hand"). That didn't bother Sei, who was well versed in the Chinese classics (she loved reminding any jumped-up male courtiers of that, too). Hiragana allowed her a tone of warm, witty intimacy – and it is that candidness that helps her words come alive all these centuries later, even if, as she claimed, they wound up in public view by accident:

> *I have written in this book things I have seen and thought, in the long idle hours spent at home, without ever dreaming that others would see it. Fearing that some of my foolish remarks could well strike others as excessive and objectionable, I did my best to keep it secret, but despite all my intentions I'm afraid it has come to light.*[32]

Her loss is our gain.

CAROLINA MARIA DE JESUS

ard is the bread that we eat. Hard is the bed on which we sleep. Hard is the life of the *favelado*."³³ These were the words of Carolina Maria de Jesus (1914–1977), a 46-year-old Brazilian writer who became her country's first black author, and the first from one of its poverty-stricken *favelas* to boot. Her diary, *Quarto de Despejo: Diário de uma Favelada* (released in English as *Child of the Dark: The Diary of Carolina Maria de Jesus*), sold out of its 10,000-copy print run over three days in 1960. It was translated into a dozen languages overseas and sold in 40 countries. Less than a decade later, however, Carolina was photographed on the street, gathering scrap paper to sell – right back where she started.

Born to a farmhand single mother in rural Brazil, Carolina was not a willing student; she had to be coerced with slaps to attend elementary school and only managed to finish second grade. By 23, she was homeless in São Paulo, where she quickly whizzed through a succession of jobs working as a maid to richer white families. Once she had become pregnant by a Portuguese sailor, however, she was tossed aside by her would-be suitor and her employer alike. (She maintained that she didn't like cleaning up after people anyway.)

In 1947, six months pregnant and penniless, Carolina travelled to Canindé, one of the city's ever-expanding slums, built a shack out of planks and tin cans with her bare hands and stayed there. When her baby was born, she scavenged for scrap paper on the street, with a burlap bag in one hand and the child tied to her back. "On good days I would make twenty-five or thirty cents," she wrote in *Child of the Dark*. "Some days I made nothing."

She had two more children and was left to raise them alone, trying her best to stave off their hunger at the expense of her own gnawing stomach. The diary helped: "I would lie on the bed and start to worry about the next day," she wrote. "I was so nervous about my children that many times I'd vomit, but there was nothing there but bile. Then I'd get up, light the lamp, and write."

Sometime around April 1958, Carolina met a rookie journalist called Audálio Dantas who had travelled to Canindé to report on a newly opened playground. A fight had broken out between drunken men and some local children over the swings. Tall and proud, Carolina had little patience for injustice; her neighbours called her Dona ("Madam") Carolina on account of her supposed airs. "If you continue mistreating these children," she screamed at the men, "I'm going to put all your names in my book!"

After some convincing, Caroline agreed to show Audálio this mysterious book of hers – or rather, the 26 notebooks she'd filled over the last three years with her personal recollections and reflections. Audálio went on to publish an excerpt from the diary in the next day's papers. "I am not bringing you a newspaper story but a revolution,"[34] he declared in the newspaper. Carolina's words shamed and stirred the country, illuminating the abysmal poverty that stalked its *favelas*. She wrote of scavenging through garbage for food, of men and women fainting in the street from hunger and of the despair of failing to provide for her children. "How horrible is it to see a child eat and ask: 'Is there more?' This word 'more' keeps ringing in the mother's head as she looks in the pot and doesn't have any more,"[35] she wrote.

When Audálio was appointed to head up the São Paulo bureau of Brazil's most popular magazine, *O Cruzeiro*, he used his platform to publish weekly excerpts from Carolina's notebooks, and helped Carolina to finally publish them all as a book. "But I did not rewrite," he said. "The words and ideas are Carolina's. All I did was edit."[36] On the day of its release, Carolina autographed 600 books at one bookshop alone as a thousand-strong crowd waited to buy a copy – even a state senator showed up. (She signed his with the message: "I hope that you give the poor people what they need and stop putting all the tax money into your own pocket.")

"When I first gave my manuscript to Brazilian editors they laughed at this poor Negro woman with calloused hands who wore rags and

only had two years schooling," she said in one TV interview. "They told me I should write on toilet paper."[37] Still, fame wasn't kind to Carolina. On the day she moved her children out of the *favela*, they were attacked by angry locals with stones. When she moved into her dream home – a modest brick house in a lower middle-class neighbourhood – her new neighbours ostracized her family.

Her next two books sold badly, and her publishers forced her to use her quickly dwindling finances to pay for her final book. Audálio, whose fortunes had risen in tandem with hers, attempted to steer her career, but Carolina wanted her independence. "I wanted to appear over the radio, to sing, to be an actress," she said. "I became furious with Audálio's control over me, rejecting everything, canceling my project."[38]

Even as her diary continued to sell overseas, she was cheated out of her royalties. Her life was comfortable enough compared to the *favela* – after selling her home, she was able to move to the countryside and grow and sell vegetables and fruit – but it wasn't the salad days of a bestselling author, either. She died of respiratory failure in 1977 and was buried in a paupers' cemetery.

"Oh, São Paulo!" she cried in *Child of the Dark*. "A queen that vainly shows her skyscrapers that are her crown of gold. All dressed up in velvet and silk but with cheap stockings underneath – the *favela*."[39] Carolina was the voice of that *favela* – but like many of its occupants, her voice ultimately went unheard by her city.

hen 19th-century author Shen Shanbao (1808–1862) was a child in Hangzhou, China, her mother, Wu Shiren, was known for her poetry, but she never found the time or freedom to pursue it as a career. "Wait till the burden on my shoulders is lighter," she promised her eldest daughter, "then I will go through my old works, and if there are some good ones, it would not be too late to have them printed."[40]

There were other considerations, too; Shanbao's father, a low-ranking provincial magistrate, had committed suicide when she was only 11 years old. The pressures of raising three young children on her own meant that Shiren stopped writing as much, and she died in 1832 without ever getting the chance to go over her old poems or produce a book.

When Shanbao entered her thirties, she found a way to revive the memory of her beloved mother's work. Over the course of two volumes, she produced a staggering work called *Mingyuan shihua* ("Remarks on Poetry of Notable Women") – a behemoth of biography and literature that collected the biographies and examples of the work of 500 women writers from the late Ming and Qing dynasties, her mother included. Over 1,300 poems were included in the text, including one by her mother, written as Shanbao was leaving home in 1828 to seek her fortune in another city. "You have the ambition of an extraordinary man," her mother wrote. "So I look upon you as a filial son."[41]

And Shanbao did have big dreams. In China, the ability to write and recite poetry had always been prized as a mark of intellect – Tang dynasty-era civil service applicants were routinely asked to compose verse as part of the notoriously difficult imperial examinations. In the 19th century, Chinese women were also beginning to pursue it as a career in its own right. If you could write as well as draw, you could travel the country making a living as a poet and painter. Thanks to her talent, Shanbao was able to provide for her family and her

younger siblings, even as she journeyed farther and farther from home, writing in 1832:

Since childhood I've indulged in reciting poetry,

and in daubing and plastering a stroke here and there.

Then I started to paint,

All the while just to amuse myself.

Who would have known that something done for pleasure

Would turn into a scheme for making a living? [42]

But the death of her mother was only part of a chain of losses in what she later termed as "ten years of broken-heartedness";[43] her little sister had already died at the age of 17, and then her brother followed in 1833, a year after her mother. In the midst of their grief, Shanbao was determined to give her family the burial they deserved. She scrimped and saved for a year so that they could be buried in a family plot, along with some other deceased relatives. "Eight coffins buried at once my heart has no more regrets. / With bare hands I didn't expect it would be ever achieved,"[44] she wrote of the bittersweet achievement.

By 1842, Shanbao's work was being praised by her peers for its elegance and virtuosity. But the double whammy of two further goodbyes, to a close friend and her foster mother, had left the poet "very much depressed and at loose ends".[45] *Remarks on Poetry of Notable Women* was the result of her melancholy, written over the course of five years. In her preface, Shanbao noted that all the histories of poetry that she'd read had a glaring lack of women – an omission that left very much to be desired, particularly for Shanbao, who had spent her twenties and thirties amassing a glittering literary circle of talented female poets and friends.

"In my humble opinion," she wrote, "women's learning is different from that of the male literati, and the transmission of women's work is more difficult than that of male scholars. The fact of the matter is, literati put all their energy into studying the classics and histories from childhood and on the side they study poetry and rhyme-prose. They have fathers and older brothers to teach them, and teachers and friends with whom to discuss."[46]

Women, she argued, lacked the necessary freedom, social connections or upbringing to truly devote themselves to it. "If she is born into a noble family or prominent lineage, and has a father or elder brother and their teachers and friends who appreciate poetry, it might be easier for her work to be transmitted widely. But if she is born into a poor home, or married to a village bumpkin, I don't know how many of these women would be sunk into oblivion and never heard of. I feel deeply for them."

Though *Remarks on Poetry of Notable Women* focuses mainly on middle-and upper-class poets like herself, Shanbao made sure to also include working-class women, such as peasants and cooks. Many of her profiles pause to include autobiographical nods to acknowledge her personal connection to their poems, be it a shared birthplace or a common acquaintance. Today, these two volumes provide an invaluable portrait of what it meant to be a woman writer in late imperial China. "My intention," Shanbao announced, "is to preserve their broken lines and scattered pieces." In that, she certainly succeeded.

t the turn of the 19th century, the word "transgender" didn't exist, let alone the diagnosis of gender dysphoria. There was, however Lili Elvenes, better known as Lili Elbe (1882–1931) – a LGBTQI pioneer and memoirist who was among the first in the world to seek gender reassignment surgery, and the first to document her experiences, with her memoirs *Man into Woman: The First Sex Change.*

Billed as "the true and remarkable transformation of the painter Einar Wegener",[47] the autobiography was published after Lili's untimely demise and assembled from her correspondence and diaries, as well as the records of her friends and ex-wife Gerda Wegener. "I am convinced that it is my moral duty to make my 'Confessions' public, in order to teach people not to judge,"[48] Lili wrote in 1931. She died just a few months later, the victim of an operation gone wrong.

Designated male at birth in Denmark, Lili (then called Einar Magnus Andreas Wegener) was often taken for a girl and was bullied on account of her "girl's voice",[49] prompting her to fake a "proper youthful bass".[50] "Looking back on things now," Lili later wrote, "it seems as if my childish voice was my first dissimulation."[51]

In 1903, Lili met Gerda at art school in Copenhagen, and they married a year later. Both became successful artists, Lili as a landscape painter and Gerda as a portraitist and illustrator. When Gerda's model, an actress named Anna Larson, dropped out of a sitting, Lili was press-ganged into Anna's clothes as a substitute. "You know, Andreas, you were certainly a girl in a former existence, or else Nature has made a mistake with you this time,"[52] Anna told Lili afterward. It was Anna who bestowed the name Lili on her that night, and Lili, Gerda and Anna celebrated her rechristening as something Lili later described as an "extravagant joke, a genuine accident of the studio". She began presenting as a woman and even became Gerda's muse, appearing in her wife's art as a glamorous Art Nouveau diva, a chain-smoking card-player, or, simply and sweetly, with her arms wrapped around her spouse.

The paintings were the making of Gerda; she received an invitation abroad to show her Lili portraits in Paris. But Lili's work and mental health were suffering – the only thing that buoyed her spirits was when she was able to dress as Lili. "The power or desire to work went out of me. Everybody who had known me for years knew that I had been

an industrious person. I could not understand myself," she wrote. "But when Lili appeared, everything went well, and life was fair once more."[53]

All her doctors said that she was in perfect physical health, but Lili soon came to another conclusion: "It came about that I formed an independent opinion, to the effect that I was both man and woman in one body, and that the woman in this body was in the process of gaining the upper hand."[54] Gerda concurred. Fortunately, science was changing, and it was decisively on Lili's side. In Berlin, Dr Magnus Hirschfeld had set up the Institute for Sexual Science and was beginning to build a bold case for the true complexity of sexual and gender identity. Lili never identified as transgender – she maintained that she had shrivelled ovaries, and some believe that she may been intersex. (Her medical records at the Institute were lost when the Nazis destroyed the centre in 1933.)

In any case, Dr Hirschfeld affirmed her gender identity and Lili embarked on a series of gender-reassignment surgeries, first at the Institute and then under the knife of Kurt Warnekros, whom Lili grew to regard as her greatest champion – she even took the name Elbe after the river that runs through the valley of his city. Though Gerda continued to support Lili throughout her life, they eventually filed for divorce in 1930.

Life back in Copenhagen wasn't easy for Lili. Her female friends accepted her instantly, but her male friends shunned her – one even shuddered at holding her hand. Romance beckoned when an old friend proposed to her, but Lili had set her heart on getting a womb transplant first; she wanted to be able to have children. "Through a child I should be able to convince myself in the most unequivocal manner," she wrote, "that I have been a woman from the very beginning."[55]

This was long before the advent of immunosuppressive drugs that would allow such a far-reaching organ transplant, but Warnekros convinced Lili that the operation was possible. She died a few months afterward, before she could see her book in print. It is written in a mix of first and third person, and she never identifies herself with Andreas, the pseudonymous name she used instead of Einar. "Should I write a preface to the book, to explain why," she wrote, "when speaking of Andreas, I always use the third person, as in a novel? But, my friend, what other form of narrative could I have chosen?"[56]

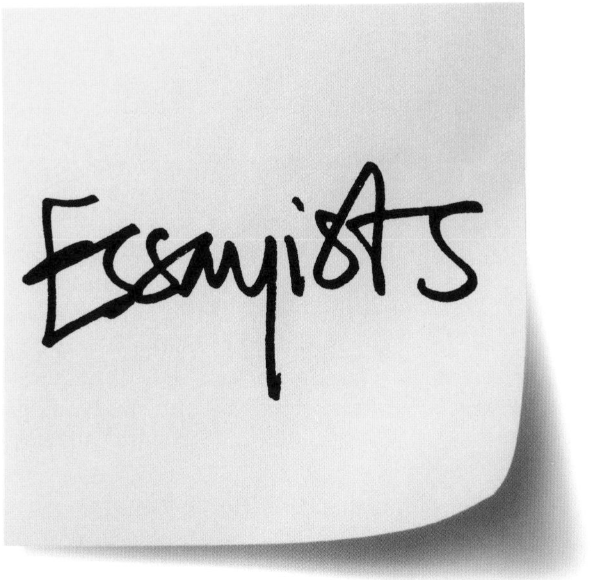
Essayists

JANE ANGER

or centuries, women were told that rage is unbecoming; that to lose one's temper is to become a hag, a nag, a bitch – or all three. The ancient Greek playwright Euripides pretty much summed up the prevailing wisdom of the age when he put these words in a female character's mouth in *Andromache*: "No man ever yet hath discovered aught to cure a woman's venom, which is far worse than viper's sting or scorching flame; so terrible a curse are we to mankind."[1]

But toward the tail end of the 16th century, a remarkable English essayist, Jane Anger (*c.*1560–*c.*1600), emerged from the Elizabethan Age, and the pamphlet she produced in 1589 was a pure and undistilled scream of rage.

In the opening pages of *Jane Anger her Protection for Women. To defend them against the Scandalous Reportes*, she greets her readers and gets down to business:

Fie on the falshoode of men, whose minds goe oft a madding, & whose tongues can not so soone bee wagging, but straight they fall a railing. Was there ever any so abused, so slaundered, so railed upon, or so wickedly handeled underservedly, as are we women?[2]

With these words, Jane launched into a full-blown treatise on gender inequality, railing against the wickedness of men and their moral hypocrisy. She didn't bother with disguising the fact that her writing was fuelled by righteous indignation. "Shall not Anger stretch the vaines of her braines, the stringes of her fingers, and the listes of her modestie, to answere their Surfeitings?"

Jane asks rhetorically, before answering her own question: "Yes truely."[3]

The Elizabethan Age frequently saw men writing pamphlets to propose, spread and denounce new ideas and philosophies – or, in the case of the male writer who inspired Jane's outrage, to make a dig at women. *Her Protection for Women* is thought to be the first known work in English to defend the female gender, and Jane among the first major female polemicists writing in the English language.

"They suppose that there is not one amongst us who can, or dare reproove their slanders and false reproches: their slaunderous tongues are so short, and the time wherin they have lavished out their wordes freely, hath bene so long, that they know we cannot catch hold of them to pull them out, and they think we wil not write to reproove their lying lips,"[4] Jane sneers. In other words: Guess what, buddy – you've met your match.

It is thought that Jane's tract may have been written in response to a pamphlet called *Boke his Surfeyt in love*, printed by a publisher known as Thomas Orwin. All copies of this work have been lost, but it's easy enough to guess some of its subject matter from Jane's own responses. On women's apparent lustfulness, she writes: "If we cloath our selves in sackcloth, and trusse up our haire in dishclouts, Venerians wil nevertheles pursue their pastime. If we hide our breastes, it must be with leather, for no cloath can keep their long nailes out of our bosomes…our eies cause them to look lasciviously, & why? because they are geven to lecherie."[5]

It's a sentiment that will strike a chord with anybody familiar with the line "look at what she was wearing – she was asking for it". In a 16th-century take on slut-shaming, Jane also argued that men sought to absolve their own lust by blaming women with "slanderous speaches against our sex". She even seeks to rehabilitate Eve, the original temptress herself, by proposing that Adam – and all his male descendants – couldn't survive without help from women. "GOD making woman of mans fleshe, that she might bee purer then he, doth evidently showe, how far we women are more excellent then men," Jane writes. "Our bodies are fruitefull, wherby the world encreaseth, and our care wonderful, by which man is preserved. From woman sprang mans salvation."[6]

The true identity of Jane Anger remains unknown; one academic theorized that her last name may have been an Anglicization of the French surname Anjou. Some have ploughed through records to unearth a few real-life Jane or Joan Angers of the time, though none of the contenders quite matches up to the fiery author of *Her Protection for Women*. Others have even suggested that Jane may have been a pseudonym for a man. It is likely, however, that the mystery woman simply selected a pseudonym that truthfully encompassed the emotion she wished to express. She was Anger by name, and angry by nature.

ALICE DUNBAR-NELSON

lice Dunbar-Nelson's (1875–1935) obituary would have infuriated her. When she died in 1935, a Philadelphia newspaper ran her obituary with the headline "Alice Ruth Moore's 2 Husbands / First, a Volatile Genius; Second, a Calm Newsman"[7], before going on to note a contemporary's recollection of the "Wife of a Poet" borrowing an ice-cream freezer.

After all, she had only stayed with her first husband – the celebrated poet Paul Laurence Dunbar – for four years, and had married "calm newsman" Robert J Nelson when she was 41. Still, it wouldn't have surprised her – there was a reason she held onto Dunbar's last name, even after their separation and his death. As a multiracial woman who proudly identified as black, the author, activist and essayist was used to battling the prevailing sexism and racism of her century. She wasn't going to say no if using her famous ex-husband's last name gave her an advantage.

Born in New Orleans, Alice was the daughter of a former slave turned seamstress and a sailor. Her mixed-race heritage and auburn hair meant that people sometimes mistook her for a white woman, leading her to a complicated relationship with her own complexion. "White enough to pass for white," she once wrote, "but with a darker family background, a real love for the mother race, and no desire to be numbered among the white race."[8] She was tormented by bullies and taunted with cries of "half-white nigger"[9] on the playground, even from a black girl she considered her friend.

When Alice published her first book of short stories and poetry at 20, her racial ambiguity helped her to enter places that were ordinarily barred to other people of African–American heritage. There were moments of humour, too;

she was twice kicked off a segregated train carriage for black travellers "because the conductor insisted that I was a white woman".[10] Alice returned to the theme of identity many times over the course of her literary career, though she sometimes cloaked it in metaphor to make it more palatable for publishers. In one short story, she writes of her protagonist Sister Josepha: "In a flash she realized the deception of the life she would lead, and the cruel self-torture of wonder at her own identity. Already, as if in anticipation of the world's questionings, she was asking herself, 'Who am I? What am I?'"[11]

It was her first book, *Violets and Other Tales*, that caught Paul Laurence Dunbar's eye. After a courtship sweetly conducted over letters, they married in 1898 and settled in New York, where they plunged into the explosive cultural movement that became known as the Harlem Renaissance (*see* pages 182–3). Paul, however, drank heavily and was a serial cheater, and their marriage soon crumbled. But though her second marriage to Robert J Nelson lasted until her death, she could never be accused of being a prude. She had a passionate, short-lived affair with a man who was 12 years younger, and she had multiple relationships with women, penning a sonnet to one declaring of their liaison: "I had not thought to ope that secret room."[12]

Alice was never able to make a full-time career out of her writing. She was constantly juggling her time as an author, speaker and campaigner for black women's suffrage and the anti-lynching cause with her full-time gig as a teacher. "Lots of irons in the fire," she wrote in her diary of her many commitments, "but where is the deliverance from my House of Bondage?"[13] Even when travelling the country to give lectures on poetry and the African–American experience, she found herself haunted by the spectre of her late husband: "My talk on the 'Negro's Literary Reaction to American Life' apparently

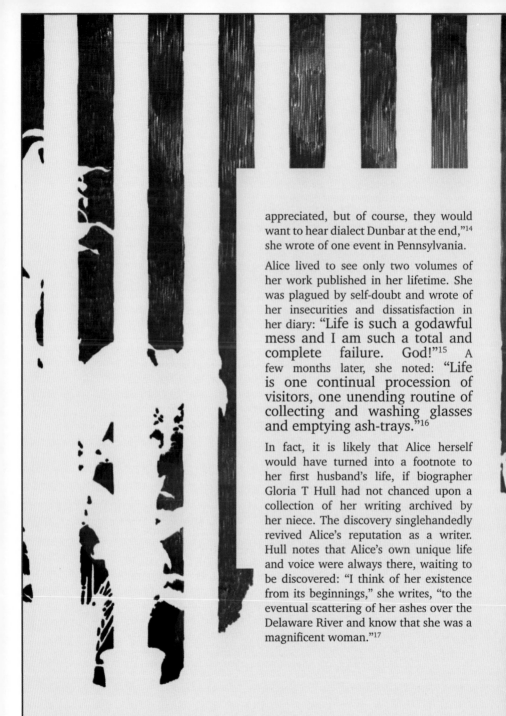

appreciated, but of course, they would want to hear dialect Dunbar at the end,"[14] she wrote of one event in Pennsylvania.

Alice lived to see only two volumes of her work published in her lifetime. She was plagued by self-doubt and wrote of her insecurities and dissatisfaction in her diary: "Life is such a godawful mess and I am such a total and complete failure. God!"[15] A few months later, she noted: "Life is one continual procession of visitors, one unending routine of collecting and washing glasses and emptying ash-trays."[16]

In fact, it is likely that Alice herself would have turned into a footnote to her first husband's life, if biographer Gloria T Hull had not chanced upon a collection of her writing archived by her niece. The discovery singlehandedly revived Alice's reputation as a writer. Hull notes that Alice's own unique life and voice were always there, waiting to be discovered: "I think of her existence from its beginnings," she writes, "to the eventual scattering of her ashes over the Delaware River and know that she was a magnificent woman."[17]

MARIANNA FLORENZI-WADDINGTON

t was in 1864 that Marianna Florenzi-Waddington (1802–1870) celebrated her 62nd birthday by publishing *Essays on Psychology and Logic*, a volume of essays that tackled one of the most pressing issues that concern both ministers of faith and philosophers alike: the immortality of the soul.

Marianna was the perfect writer to attack such a lofty topic. The distinguished scholar from Ravenna, Italy, was adventurous enough to champion heretic philosophers and impenetrable philosophy alike, and she had already devoted much of her life to studying and translating the intellectually punishing work of German thinkers like Friedrich Schelling. It was thanks to Marianna's flair for translation that their liberal ideas got a hearing in Italy at all.

Born in 1802 to the aristocratic Bacinetti family, Marianna was packed off to nearby Faenza to study under a philosopher named Torrigiani. She was, however, made to leave school at the age of 15 to marry a fellow member of the nobility, the Marquis Ettore Florenzi of Perugia, and she bore him two children. It was no love match – the Marquis was once described as *piccolo, brutto, vecchio* ("little, ugly, old"), and to make matters worse, he was about thrice the age of his teenage bride.

But Marianna was not the type to sink into despair; the newly minted Marchesa carried on with her intellectual activities, becoming one of the first women to read natural sciences at the University of Perugia. When she was 18, she met Ludwig I of Bavaria – he was then Crown Prince Ludwig, first in line to the Bavarian throne – and began a lengthy, decades-long correspondence, consisting of more than 4,000 letters.

Some historians believe that their friendship was purely intellectual and platonic, but others have argued that, given Ludwig's admiration for women of great beauty and charm, romance was inevitable. Not for nothing did one of the pavilions in his summer palace become known as the *Schönheitengalerie,* or the "Gallery of Beauties" – it was where he hung paintings of the doe-eyed women he considered the world's most beautiful. Two hundred years on, Marianna's portrait still hangs there.

Make no mistake, though – the Marchesa was not your typical Bavarian palace-approved beauty. Leading intellectuals gathered at her home to discuss science, and an endless parade of philosophers lined up to exchange letters with her, hoping to pick her brain for insights. Her second husband, an Englishman named Evelino Waddington, was so taken with her that he even took Italian citizenship. By making Kant, Leibniz and Hegel comprehensible, Marianna almost singlehandedly popularized the German philosophy of idealism in her country. She astounded Schelling with her knowledge and was judged so impressive that she was asked to translate some of his unpublished manuscripts.

At a time when Roman Catholicism reigned supreme, Marianna also wasn't afraid to ruffle feathers in the Church – her 1850 work *Some Reflections on Socialism and Communism* was added to the Index Librorum Prohibitorum, the infamous register of books deemed threatening to the Christian faith. She championed Giordano Bruno, the Italian heretic priest who had espoused Copernican science and was burned at the stake for it by the Inquisition in 1600. Marianna read widely and voraciously; one of her treatises on the human soul cited everything from Hegelian philosophy to the Bhagavad Gita. In *Essays on Psychology and Logic,* she applied Hegel to spiritual matters, arguing that the immortality of the soul was a necessary component to his logic. "I follow the impulse of my spirit and take delight in dealing with philosophical topics," she once wrote of her approach, "rising in desire to the high places of wisdom that we mortals can still reach only fleetingly."[18]

Marianna lived to be 68, and followed up *Essays* with four more treatises, in which she applied her intellect to everything from political theory to natural philosophy. Nothing was more important to her than the constant drive toward further enlightenment – whatever the love affairs or mishaps along the way. "We are happiest," she informed a cousin in a letter, "when the Idea of ideas shines so brightly upon us that it permits our spirit, impassioned and inflamed, to move for a few moments to the supernal spaces, and filled with desire, and love, to rejoin that eternal existence in union with which we taste a little of the beatitude that is the life of the Absolute, towards which we feel an inborn and irresistible drive."[19]

n 1935, May Ziade (1886–1941), also written Ziadeh, was languishing in a psychiatric institution in Beirut, Lebanon, where she would remain for four years. The Lebanese–Palestinian author and translator had sunk into depression with the shock of twin losses: the death of her parents and the death of her great love, the Arab–American poet Khalil Gibran. Instead of offering sympathy, her relatives sought to seize her estate by committing her to an asylum. It was a dramatic change from her previous life as a leading Arab intellectual and essayist.

As a girl, May had inherited a love of writing from her Lebanese father Elias Ziade, the founding editor of the Egyptian newspaper *al-Mahrūsah*. She adored the Romantic poets and wrote fondly of Byron, whom she described as a "poet of violence and sweetness". "Did Byron ever dream," she wondered, "that a Lebanese girl would spend with him or with some of his works, long, lonely hours in the woods of Lebanon?"[20]

At the age of 25, she published a collection of poetry in French entitled *Fleurs de rêve*, and followed her father into journalism. Her education at a French convent boarding school in Lebanon, followed by a degree in modern languages, served her well. In her body of work from this time, leading essays and articles on gender equality and political governance sit next to short stories, novels and plays, which in turn were complemented by her Arabic translations of European authors like Arthur Conan Doyle.

May issued passionate calls to advance the status of women in poetry and prose, and spoke publicly on the issue. "The duties required of woman are numerous indeed," she wrote in an essay titled "Women and Work".

"She has to be good-looking, dainty, smooth-tempered...
She has to bear children, take care of their physical,
moral and intellectual growth. She has to know the
principles of economy and of successful housekeeping...
Thus she has to perform the functions of a minister of
the interior, a minister of foreign affairs, of education, of
communications, of colonies, etc. All those responsibilities
which are distributed among a select group of men are
shouldered by a single woman, and yet we keep saying
that she is weak!"[21]

Around 1913, May founded a salon at her Cairo family
home that blossomed into a nexus of Arab literary culture,
attracting numerous distinguished artists and writers
of the time. Unlike other salons, men and women of all
backgrounds and religions mixed freely. "May's salon
was democratic; in the sense that it was open
to various classes of intellectuals and to literary
men and women of different nationalities:
Egyptians, Lebanese, Syrians, Europeans and
others," one visitor, the scholar Taha Hussein,
remembered. "They discussed all sorts of topics, local
and international...Unique in character, this salon had a
decided influence on its habitues, who spoke highly of it in
their memoirs and their reminiscences."[22]

Unfortunately, May's reputation as the greatly admired and
charming hostess of the salon began to surpass her literary
accomplishments. The Egyptian author Abbās Mahmoud
al-Aqqād wrote approvingly of her salon and rather more
patronizingly of her appearance: "She turned the whole
world into a reception hall where beauty is not disturbed
by anything, or maybe it is her looks that resemble a
beautiful museum packed with good taste."[23]

Her mysterious relationship with Khalil Gibran, too, began to overshadow her own literary talent. Khalil lived in New York and May in Beirut; they never once met in person, though they carried on a passionate correspondence for 20 years. We have no record of May's letters – only of Khalil's. In one message, he writes: "Do you know how much I desire to receive that letter after having read a brief snatch of it – a divine fragment which arrived to announce the dawning of a new day?"[24]

May was singlehandedly responsible for introducing Khalil's work to the Arab world, and in turn fell in love with and adopted *shi'r manthur*, the Arabic style of prose poetry that he popularized. She never married, and rumours about her personal life – that she was in love with Khalil, that she was a lesbian – began to spread about her.

Only a few friends stood by her when Khalil's death and the passing of her parents catalyzed her depression and sent her to the asylum. It was four years before a long-running press campaign to free her finally paid off, and she was released. May continued to write in her final years, but her reputation had been irretrievably damaged. The great woman responsible for moulding Arab literature had long passed into the realm of the forgotten. Before she died, May simply said: "I hope that after my death someone will do me justice."[25]

SHULAMITH HAREVEN

hough Shulamith Hareven (1930–2003) was born in chilly Warsaw in 1930, her life began in earnest ten years later, when she fled the Holocaust with her family for Mandatory Palestine. "Born in Europe, I spent my time there, in an obscure impatience, as if it were all a mistake, a confinement, like a wretched marriage – till I first saw strong light on the rocky hedges of a mountain, a stooping summer olive tree, a well carved in stone – and I knew that was it," she once wrote. "I had arrived at something deep, palpable, ancient, the womb of the world, in which virtually everything has been and will be created."[31]

Shulamith and her parents were among the thousands of Jewish people who sought refuge in the British-controlled territory, which was partitioned to create the state of Israel in 1948. Though Shulamith joined the Haganah (the underground military organization that later formed the basis of the Israel Defense Forces) and served as a combat medic during the 1948 Arab–Israeli War, she became her country's unfaltering voice of conscience and one of its strongest advocates for peace.

As a war correspondent for the Israeli newspaper *Yediot Aharonot*, she filed first-hand reports from the front lines of the War of Attrition and the Yom Kippur War that revealed the desperation and destruction of the conflicts. "I've never lived for long in a quiet place and I've been shot at since I was 8,"[32] she wryly told an interviewer from the *New York Times*.

Though once described as an "ardent Zionist",[33] Shulamith's own work and politics defied easy categorization. Her love of her adopted country and the surrounding region of the Levant – loosely encompassing Syria, Palestine, Jordan, Cyprus and Israel – led her to a shared and communal identity with her neighbours and to celebrate "the colourblind pluralism that sees no racial, ethnic or religious differences".[34]

In 1990, she summed up her identity for the benefit of an audience at the Barbican in London: "I am a Levantine."[35] Despite this,

she maintained that her personal life – and her past as a Holocaust survivor – should not define her writing. She made only the occasional venture into autobiography. "Culture begins," Shulamith wrote of the contemporary impulse to reveal oneself in public, "where people recognize the difference between the private and the public."[36]

Her work as a war reporter meant that Shulamith saw the devastating consequences of Israeli settlement policy and its militarism, or, as she described it, "the total failure of common sense"[37] – Palestinian residents shunted between Gaza checkpoints, refugees languishing in camps during the First Intifada (Palestinian uprising) and "constant harassment... for its own sake, evil for its own sake".[38] She later became a spokesperson for the Peace Now movement, advocating a two-state solution to the Israeli–Palestinian conflict.

Shulamith didn't just report on her country; she also shaped its language. Over the course of her career, she published 19 books in Hebrew, including poetry, short stories, novellas, three volumes of essays and an additional English collection entitled *The Vocabulary of Peace* – many translated into different languages, including Chinese, Arabic and Spanish. For 12 years, she was the first and only woman to be inducted into the Academy of the Hebrew Language, the Israeli organization that sought to revive and modernize the ancient tongue. There, she fought for new additions to

Israel's official language to shake off any remnants of sexism, including a successful campaign to change the new Hebrew word for telephone from its feminine incarnation (*mazkira elektronit*, or "electronic secretary") to a more gender-neutral term (*meshivon*, or "answerer").

But if Shulamith was a critical voice in Israeli society, she was also one of its most utopian thinkers – dreaming of a time when the region she loved so much would know peace. "The boundaries which will determine our future are not geographic," she wrote of her country. "The true boundary is, rather, the knowledge that there is a limit to power. The respect which we need will not come through conquest by the sword: it can be obtained only through respect for others. Our ultimate hope is not for the undivided land of Israel, but for an Israel which is undivided in spirit and at peace with itself."[39]

he late 16th and 17th centuries were not kind to women in Italy. During the Counter-Reformation, as the Church tightened its grip on power, women were increasingly seen as sinful temptresses and wretched creatures. Male philosophers and writers even began debating their rightful place in society – if they deserved one at all – and nobody embodied these poisonous attitudes better than Giuseppe Passi, who published *I donneschi difetti* ("The Defects of Women") in 1599. The scholar heaped scorn on women's intelligence and warned of their feminine wiles – women, he suggested, were better off kept under lock and key by their husbands.

Passi would have been able to get away with it, too, were it not for Lucrezia Marinella (1571–1653), one of the most learned women in Italy. At a young age, the Venetian scholar had authored everything from religious poetry to philosophical commentary, including an epic poem named *La Colomba sacra*, which followed the story of a Christian woman who would rather martyr herself than abandon her religion.

Lucrezia didn't want to let the misogyny of her male peers slide, especially as part of Passi's argument was that women also made rotten poets. In 1600, Lucrezia published her blistering treatise in defence of her gender: *The Nobility and Excellence of Women, and the Defects and Vices of Men.* (The vices of men took up 35 chapters.)

Lucrezia had never written anything like it before, though a quick glance at her upbringing confirms that she was uniquely placed to write it. Her father, Giovanni Marinelli, was a distinguished natural philosopher and physician who had published texts about women's issues and health when Lucrezia was just a girl. He had encouraged her to read books by women and to speak up at the many intellectual meetings he organized at home for the great and good of Venice. Where most girls were shipped off to either a nunnery or the marital bed when they came of age, Lucrezia managed to put off marriage until her fifties, crediting her singlehood as the reason she was able to pursue her studies.

In *The Nobility and Excellence of Women*, not only did Lucrezia tackle Passi's criticism of women head-on – she also squared up to ancient philosophers like Aristotle and contemporary writers like Torquato Tasso and Boccaccio, seeing these men as part of an unbroken chain of misogynist thought.

"In this treatise of mine," she wrote in her introduction, "I want to show that the feminine sex is nobler and more excellent than that of men, and I want this truth to shine in everyone's mind. And I hope to show this by means of reasons and examples that every man, even the stubborn ones, will be obliged to confirm with his own mouth."[40]

Lucrezia didn't just mount a defence of her gender by pointing out the philosophical inconsistencies and fallacies in the "false objections of slanderers".[41] She wanted no less than to argue for the superiority of women themselves, and cited everything from Plato's *The Republic* to contemporary philosophy. She even devoted an entire chapter to "Women Learned and Knowledgeable in Many Arts" to rebuke any man who believed that women were incapable of learning.

"Women are much nobler in their activities than men; if they do not exercise, or if they do not partake in this, it is because they are forbidden by men who are being motivated by their obstinate ignorance being, as they are, cocksure that women are not good at learning," she wrote. "I would like such individuals to make this experiment: to exercise a boy and a girl of the same age and of the same good nature and talent in letters and arms. They would see in a very short time that the girl would much more quickly learn than the boy, and better, that she would beat him by a great margin."[42]

The Nobility and Excellence of Women proved so popular that it was reissued a year after its release. And indeed its greatest success lay in the effect that it had on its intended target, Giuseppe Passi. He began furiously back-pedalling on some of his views and even recanted his woman-hating past in a new tract, *Dello stato maritale* ("On the Marital State"). The content of the first part of this treatise began by praising women for their beauty, learning and virtue – and affirming that they were nothing less than equal to men.

Journalists & Editors

ne woman dripped belladonna into her own eyes to dilate her pupils, and then pretended to faint in the street. Another, in Chicago, feigned pregnancy and went looking for an illegal abortion. A woman in New York faked hysteria to get committed to a madhouse. They infiltrated dismal jails, opium dens, uncaring public hospitals and exploitative factories and sweatshops. In the late 19th century, the Girl Stunt Reporters (c. 1880s–1890s) did it all – and under pseudonyms, to boot.

Toward the tail end of the 19th century, a different breed of newspapers emerged out of the cramped, industrial cities of the US. Publications like the *New York World* traded on sensationalism and headline-grabbing stunts, and, in the sneering words of one comic weekly, this "yellow journalism" had zero "sense of decency and respect for the rights of citizens, either public or private; it exploits everything that is sensational and vile, blows its own trumpet continually and claims to be the greatest force for good in the community".[1] Yet some of the tabloid antics of these publications laid the groundwork for modern-day investigative reporting – and in those days, there was no front-page story more attention-grabbing than those filed by daredevils like Nellie Bly, Eva Gay, Annie Laurie and their contemporaries.

Pennsylvania-born and New York-based Nellie (real name Elizabeth Cochrane) was the pioneer of the field. In a two-part series, "Ten Days in a Mad-house", the *World* reporter documented her success at tricking doctors into committing her to Blackwell's Island Asylum and recounted the dire conditions she witnessed there, from the beatings to the abusive attendants. One patient told her that the doctors injected so much morphine into patients that it was enough to drive people mad to begin with. "I have watched patients stand and gaze longingly toward the city they in all likelihood will never enter again," Nellie wrote. "It means liberty and life; it seems so near, and yet heaven is not further from hell."[2]

"Ten Days in a Mad-house" caused an uproar, prompting a grand jury investigation and the addition of $850,000 to the budget of the Department of Public Charities and Corrections to improve its mental health care. It also sparked an arms race between the *World* and its competitors – now every paper wanted its own Nellie, and there was no shortage of female reporters who stepped up to the plate, thrilled to escape the society pages and get a shot at the front page.

In Minnesota, *St. Paul Globe* stunt reporter Eva McDonald Valesh (a.k.a. Eva Gay) joined female workers at garment and mattress factories to expose horrific working conditions and low wages, with "air so thick with dust and lint from the bags that I could hardly see".[3] One labourer told Eva: "We pretty much freeze here in winter; our hands and feet get numb with the cold and we can't get warm."[4] The women went on strike less than a month after her piece came out.

In San Francisco, Winifred Sweet Black (alias Annie Laurie) pretended to pass out in public and got herself admitted to a negligent public hospital. She documented every step of the way there, from its improvised ambulance (a shoddy police wagon) to her discharge after an emetic of mustard and hot water was poured down her throat. In the Midwest, it was an anonymous female journalist who produced America's first-ever study of illegal abortion for the *Chicago Times*. Credited as "Girl Reporter", she visited over two hundred doctors to investigate the underground abortion industry in Chicago, where unscrupulous doctors promised desperate women the chance to terminate their pregnancy at a cost.

These women exposed the social ills that plagued their cities and prompted reform and change at a state level. But as

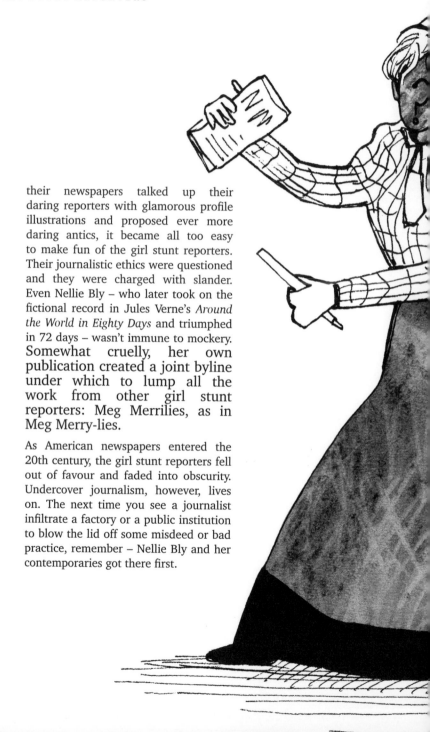

their newspapers talked up their daring reporters with glamorous profile illustrations and proposed ever more daring antics, it became all too easy to make fun of the girl stunt reporters. Their journalistic ethics were questioned and they were charged with slander. Even Nellie Bly – who later took on the fictional record in Jules Verne's *Around the World in Eighty Days* and triumphed in 72 days – wasn't immune to mockery. Somewhat cruelly, her own publication created a joint byline under which to lump all the work from other girl stunt reporters: Meg Merrilies, as in Meg Merry-lies.

As American newspapers entered the 20th century, the girl stunt reporters fell out of favour and faded into obscurity. Undercover journalism, however, lives on. The next time you see a journalist infiltrate a factory or a public institution to blow the lid off some misdeed or bad practice, remember – Nellie Bly and her contemporaries got there first.

n 1924, Liveright Publishing hailed a brand-new voice in African–American literature: "There's something new under the sun, and it is *There Is Confusion*."[5] It was a novel from Jessie Redmon Fauset (1882–1961) about the struggles of middle- and upper-class black people. It earned her comparisons to Edith Wharton, and she was later described as the "black Jane Austen".[6] With four novels and countless editorials and articles in *The Crisis* – W E B Du Bois's magazine affiliated to the NAACP (National Association for the Advancement of Colored People) – Jessie didn't just live through the explosion of black art and culture that was the Harlem Renaissance; in the words of Langston Hughes, she "midwifed"[7] it into being. All she wanted, she maintained, was to portray the "breathing-spells, in-between spaces where colored men and women work and love".[8]

Jessie was born in New Jersey in 1882. As the book-smart daughter of a Methodist reverend, Jessie was sent to Philadelphia High School for Girls, where her stellar grades earned her a scholarship to Cornell University. After she got her bachelor's degree from Cornell as its first black graduate, Jessie – armed with flawless French – went on to get a master's degree in romance languages from the University of Pennsylvania.

Jobs, however, were not forthcoming – she had to move several times over, from Philadelphia to Baltimore and then to Washington, DC, to find employment in teaching, her chosen field. When she successfully placed a few poems and short stories in *The Crisis*, however, Du Bois was impressed enough to offer her the New York-based job of literary editor. In 1919, Jessie packed her bags and departed the capital for Harlem.

In *Plum Bun*, Jessie's second novel, published in 1928, her light-skinned and white-passing protagonist Angela Murray makes a similar journey, leaving Philly behind to pursue life as an artist in Greenwich Village. She describes New York as a city of "two visages. It could offer an aspect radiant with promise or a countenance lowering and forbidding."[9] Luckily, Jessie found the former when she moved with her sister into West 142nd Street.

She turned their apartment into one of the best-known literary salons of the time, where the intellectuals, artists and activists of the Harlem Renaissance mixed and mingled. Jessie used her powerful position as literary editor to support and mentor then-emerging writers like Langston Hughes and Jean Toomer – in fact, Jessie published Hughes's very first poem. He remarked of her innumerable soirees: "There was always quite a different atmosphere from that of most other Harlem good-time gatherings…White people were seldom present there unless they were very distinguished white people, because Jessie Fauset did not feel like opening her home to mere sightseers, or faddists momentarily in love with Negro life."[10]

Jessie continued to write for *The Crisis*, contributing poems, short stories and a novella; publishing several biographies of notable black figures; and working with Du Bois on *The Brownies' Book*, a magazine for black children. "It is urgent that ambitious Negro youth be able to read of the achievements of their race," she said. "When I was a child I used to puzzle my head ruefully over the fact that in school we studied the lives of only great white people. I took it that there simply have been no great Negroes, and I was amazed when, as I grew older, I found that there were. It is a pity that Negro children should be permitted to suffer from that delusion at all."[11]

Jessie's pen shaped *The Crisis* in other, non-literary ways – she filed travel essays from her travels through post-World War I France and Italy, and reports from the Pan-African Congress of 1921. "We clasped hands with our newly found brethren and departed," she wrote glowingly of the conference, "feeling that it was good to be alive and most wonderful to be colored."[12]

By 1926, however, she had fallen out with Du Bois at *The Crisis*. At the time, her boss was in debt to her to the tune of $2,500 and hadn't paid up. Worse still, she felt that the magazine was moving away from cultural content and sidelining her literary coverage. A notice in the May issue of that year announced she was stepping down as literary editor to take a contributing editor role instead.

When Jessie sought work in publishing elsewhere, she couldn't find a company willing to take her on. If her race was a factor, she said, she could work from home – but she struggled to find anyone to take her up on the offer. Jessie returned to teaching; her next two books were less well received, and by the 1930s her work was considered too stiff and formal, its concerns too bourgeois and middle class. Yet she always held true to her maxim that there were, and always would be, those who would welcome her words: "Here is an audience waiting to hear the truth about us," she said in 1932 of being a black author writing for a black audience. "Let us who are better qualified to present that truth than any white writer, try to do so."[13]

MARIE LE JARS DE GOURNAY

hen Renaissance writer Marie Le Jars de Gournay (1565–1645) read Michel de Montaigne's *Essays* for the first time, the 18-year-old was so excited that her mother thought she should be sedated. Little did Marie know that she would meet the French philosopher himself some five years later, or that they would become so close that Montaigne grew to think of her as his *fille d'alliance* (loosely translated as "adopted daughter") and that she would be made his literary executor and editor.

Marie's widowed mother didn't believe in the education of girls, but that didn't stop her eldest daughter from teaching herself Latin or tearing through every book available to her in Gournay-sur-Aronde, the family estate. Montaigne's work singlehandedly popularized the essay form, and Marie was thrilled by it. In her words, she "began to desire knowledge, conversation and fellowship with their author more than all things in the world".[14] On the eve of her court debut in Paris in 1588, Marie heard that Montaigne was in town and sent a letter declaring her admiration for his *Essays* to his hotel, sparking a mutual friendship and correspondence that would last for the four years until his death. On their long walks together on her estate, Montaigne and Marie would talk about books and the alterations he was planning to make to his *Essays*.

That Montaigne himself respected Marie as an intellectual equal and friend was remarkable and speaks to her intelligence and trustworthiness. This was, after all, the same man who mused on friendship that "the ordinary capacity of women is inadequate for that communion and fellowship which is the nurse of this sacred bond".[15] When Montaigne died, Marie grew close to his widow Françoise

de La Chassaigne and his daughter Léonore, spending 16 months at their chateau on the border of Bordeaux and the Périgord. She was entrusted with her former mentor's legacy and, up in the round tower of his library, she edited eight new editions of *Essays*, including translating its Greek and Latin references and incorporating his new notes and amendments.

Not unlike her *père* Montaigne, Marie was determined to forge her own path as a public intellectual. "Nature has so honored me that, except for the more or less, I resemble my father," she wrote in the preface to the 1595 edition of *Essays*. "I cannot take a step, whether in writing or speaking, that I do not find myself following in his footsteps."[16]

Unfortunately, it was not a good time to be a professional female author in France. The essayist Jean-Louis Guez de Balzac himself once said to a friend that if he "were a police officer, [he] would drive back to domesticity all the women who wanted to write".[17] Marie found allies in other learned European women; Dutch scholar Anna Maria van Schurman, who spoke 14 languages, praised Marie in a Latin poem as a "great and noble-minded heroine"[18] and a "strong defender of the cause of our sex".[19] Marguerite de Valois, Queen of Navarre, bestowed on Marie a small financial stipend to take care of her needs and her library.

Yet Marie was also greeted by snobbery and ridicule. After she penned a treatise in reaction to the assassination of King Henry VI, a satirical pamphlet entitled *L'Anti-Gournay* ("Against Gournay") appeared, prompting others to jump on the bandwagon. She was viciously caricatured in plays and criticized in print. Marie was even the subject of an intensely mean-spirited hoax – three pranksters told her that King James I of England wanted to include her portrait and biography in a work on famous men and women. Marie later took them to court and, in a triumphant twist, included the text in an edition of her collected works *Les Advis, ou les Presens de la Demoiselle de Gournay* ("The Demoiselle of Gournay's Presents and Offerings").

"Is there today a more specific target for slanderers than the condition of those who love learning if they do not belong to the church or the law?" she asked in the 1641 preface to *Les Advis*. "In our epoch nothing is more stupid or ridiculous, next to poverty, than being an enlightened and learned man: except, of course, being an enlightened and learned woman, or simply aspiring, like me, to become one."[20]

Marie didn't let the mockery and scorn hold her back. She lived to be 80 and produced treatises on French literature, education, philosophy and women's rights. Education, she said, was what would ultimately liberate "the ladies oppressed by the tyranny of men" – books, in fact, much like the one she edited.

With a grandfather who was the first black owner of a newspaper in South Africa, Noni Jabavu (1919–2008) appeared destined for journalism. Her parents, however, had other plans. "A house called Tsalta, at Claremont, Cape, was where I first beheld and shook hands with the English couple who were to be my guardians in England," she wrote later, in one of her columns for South Africa's *Daily Dispatch*. "That house was where General and Mrs. Smuts lived. Its name was backwards for 'At last'."[21]

In 1933, Noni was sent away from her home in the Eastern Cape to be educated in Britain under the watchful eye of her new guardians. "At 13 I was not too well primed about the negotiations that must have gone on between my parents and my prospective loco-parents, about the life they were planning for me which I was to learn in years to come," she wrote, "[and how it] was to be a practical demonstration of the generations of friendship between families. I learned then that the plan was for me to be trained as a doctor to serve my people. But it misfired, for a medical doctor was the one thing I didn't want to be. I didn't know what I wanted to be."[22]

Instead, she enrolled briefly at the Royal Academy of Music in London and also had a stint as a film technician. During World War II, she welded bomber engine parts for the war effort. After the war she found work at the BBC as one of its few South African presenters and producers, and in 1951 she married a British film director. "I belong to two worlds with two loyalties: South Africa, where I was born, and England, where I was educated,"[23] she explained later.

Noni's marriage to a white man brought its own difficulty. Under the apartheid regime in South Africa, their mixed-race union was unlawful and he could not travel with her to her homeland. In 1955, tragedy prompted her return to the Eastern Cape – her younger brother, Tengo, had been shot dead by gangsters while he was studying medicine in Johannesburg. "When I received a cable sent by my father, I flew back to South Africa to be amongst my Bantu people, leaving my English husband behind in London,"[24] Noni wrote.

The heartbreak prompted her to write her 1960 debut novel *Drawn in Colour*. It is a skilful and tender portrait of her homecoming in a rapidly changing South Africa, and of her feelings at being trapped somewhere on the outside, looking in. "The mores that I was used to were neither purely Western nor purely Bantu," she wrote. "We were not 'black Europeans', yet I saw how we were not 'white Bantu' either."[25] One critic from the American journal *Kirkus Reviews* praised her "strongly flavored"[26] use of her "Xhosa language, which translates most nearly into poetic Elizabethan English".[27]

"Words are pliable," Noni noted of her native tongue, "[and] can be manipulated and therefore impregnated with subtle, often startling shades of meaning..."[28] Of the thousands who arrived for her brother's funeral in the Eastern Cape, she writes in *Drawn in Colour*:

"Child!" they said. "This news burst on us like the report of a cannon! We heard but could not believe, COULD NOT BELIEVE! Our Tengo dead so young, in his last few months of becoming a trained doctor? Oh God-in-heaven! He who would have been a precious doctor for our people, our only Tengo, of-Tengo-the-

Professor who is in turn Tengo-of-the-grand-old-one u-Mhleli,
Editor of our first newspaper-of-our-people-1884!...God gave
them to us black South Africans. Now he takes them away."[29]

When *Drawn in Colour* was published to critical acclaim in
London, Noni officially became the first black South African
woman to publish an autobiographical work. A year later,
there was another ground-breaking feat with her appointment
as editor of the London-based publication *The New Strand* –
she became the first African woman to edit a British literary
magazine. "Jamaica in January; midwinter in Menton, next April
in Alexandria," she wrote in one editorial. "My travel diary seems
bent on onomatopoeia, alliteration. Or is it bending that way
because my mother tongue is an alliterative language?"[30] *Drawn
in Colour* was reprinted five times and was also translated into
Italian; in 1963, she followed it up with another memoir of her
time in South Africa, *The Ochre People*.

In the 1970s, Noni returned to South Africa to research a
biography about her father, D D T Javabu, the famed languages
professor and former president of the All-Africa Convention
(AAC). While she was there, she followed in the footsteps of
her grandfather by becoming a columnist for the *Daily Dispatch*,
an Eastern Cape newspaper founded in 1872. However, she
never settled in her home country again – because of
her British passport and various immigration policies
at the time, she led a nomadic life, writing her books
in Uganda, Jamaica and Spain from the sanctuary of
hotel rooms and friends' homes.

Her pioneering contributions to South African literature,
however, were finally acknowledged when the ANC (African
National Congress) took power and recognized her with a lifetime
achievement award. All her life, Noni confounded expectations
– not only those of her parents, with their dreams of raising a
doctor, but also the expectations of those who could not conceive
of a black female author being so prolific and successful. "We
men," South African poet Mongane Wally Serote said of Noni,
"did not know how to relate to her. She was a woman living far
ahead of our times."[31]

DOROTHY TODD

 n 1915, Dorothy Todd (1883–1966) set sail from Liverpool to New York. The 32-year-old Englishwoman was bound for the offices of American *Vogue*, where she helped to create the magazine's British edition (or *Brogue*, as its Manhattan staffers called it). Seven years later, after acquiring the requisite training for a would-be editor, Dorothy – or Dody, as her friends and many lovers called her – became the very first editor of British *Vogue* back in London.

Dorothy may not have seemed like an obvious frontrunner to lead *Vogue*. Described as "alarmingly butch"[32] by some, she was an out-of-the-closet lesbian when many preferred to stay in; she had an illegitimate daughter, whom she passed off as her niece, by way of a one-off assignation with a mystery man; and she was just as interested in Modernist literature and art as she was into eau de Cologne and iron-grey suits with velvet collars.

During the Roaring 20s, however, Dorothy made the perfect editor. *Vogue* was still only a few decades old and had yet to establish itself as a global phenomenon; Dorothy's British incarnation was very much an ongoing experiment. And, boy, did Dody experiment – in her debut issue, the magazine made this bold declaration: *"Vogue* has no intention of confining its pages to hats and frocks. In literature, the drama, art and architecture, the same spirit of change is seen at work, and to the intelligent observer the interplay of suggestion and influence between all these things is one of the fascinations of the study of the contemporary world."[33]

Under Dorothy's leadership, the magazine became more than a compilation of trends and lifestyle tips. In one issue, readers were delighted by an emerging artist known as Pablo Picasso and his cheeky cartoons; in another, they were treated to Virginia Woolf's review of *The Tale of Genji* – she compared Murasaki Shikibu (*see* page 70) to Tolstoy and Cervantes. Victorian frills and corsets were out; dropped waists, cloche hats and winking nods to Sapphic sisters were in.

Dorothy was just as interested in "fashions of the mind"[34] as she was in clothes for the body – she threw riotous parties at her Chelsea apartment to seduce all the Bright Young Things of London's emerging Bloomsbury set into writing for the magazine. By 1923, she had also literally seduced one of *Vogue*'s rising stars – Madge Garland, a Melbourne-born receptionist who had reinvented herself behind the concierge and ascended the ranks of the magazine to become fashion editor.

At a time when writing opportunities for women were scarce, *Vogue* was the making of many a young female talent, Madge included. "I owe [Dorothy] everything," she once remarked. Dorothy's innumerous charms also saw Madge ditch her husband to move in with her boss, where she formed part of Dorothy's fashion-forward gang. On spotting Madge in the corridors, Aldous Huxley once quipped, "Are you dressed like that because you are on *Vogue* or are you on *Vogue* because you are dressed like that?"[35]

Young, cool, queer and knowingly hip – that was Dorothy Todd's *Vogue*. "If anyone should some morning unawares discover symptoms of old age creeping upon her," one editorial went, "one of the first things

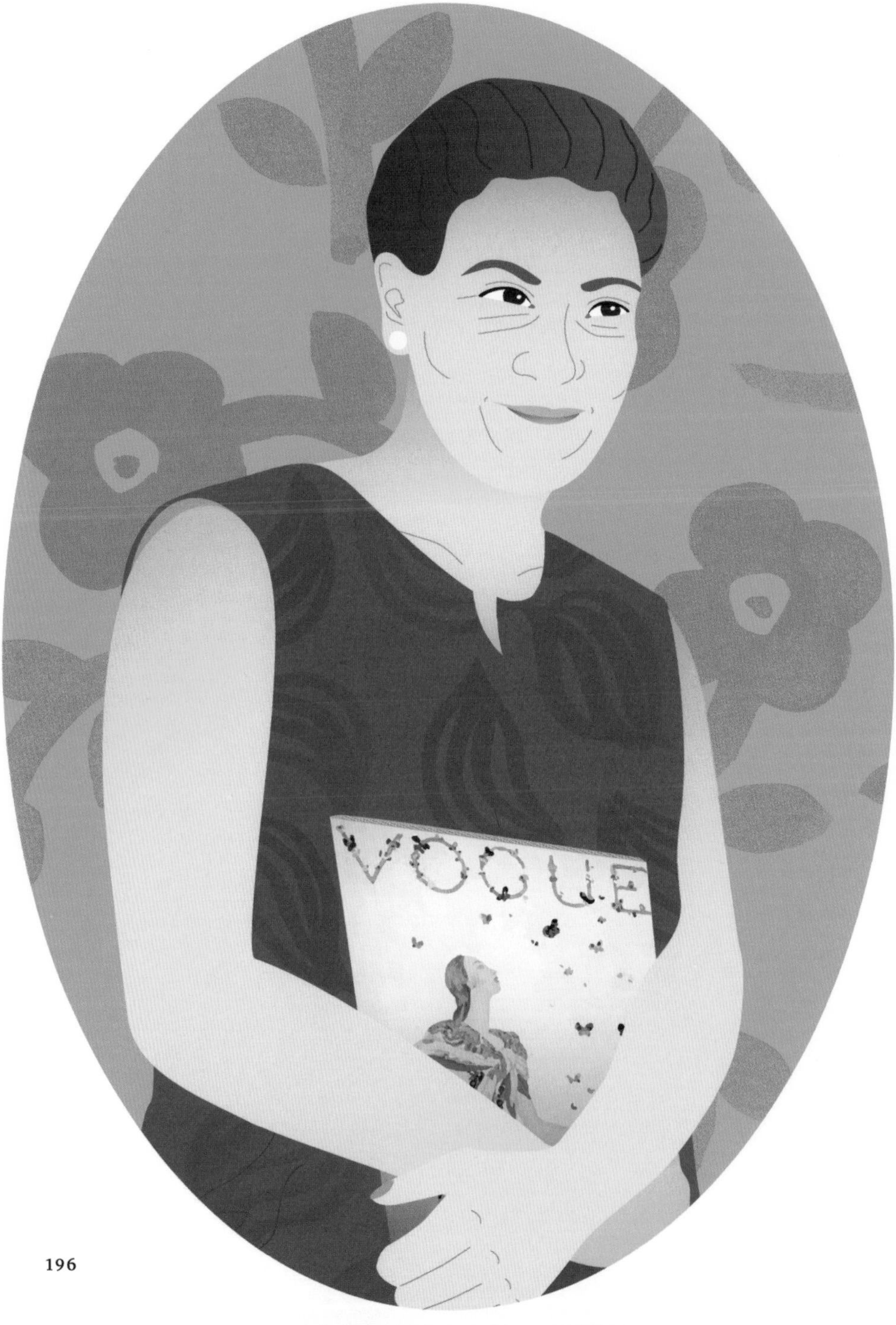
VOGUE

the patient should do is to send out for a copy of *Vogue*. This has been found efficacious in even the worst cases of confirmed middle age, and taken regularly will prevent any danger of a recurrence of the malady."[36]

By 1926, however, Dorothy's bosses were growing increasingly unhappy with her direction. *Vogue* editor-in-chief Edna Woolman Chase and publisher Condé Montrose Nast alleged that their unruly employee's highbrow aspirations were causing advertising and print sales to plummet. Dorothy was unceremoniously fired, and began seeking legal advice to sue the company.

But there were other forces at work, to which the poet and *Vogue* contributor Vita Sackville-West darkly alluded in a letter: "Nast, when threatened with an action, reported that he would defend himself by attacking Todd's morals. So poor Todd is silenced, since her morals are of the classic rather than the conventional order."[37] It would be another 91 years until British *Vogue* saw another openly gay editor, in the form of Edward Enninful.

Cast adrift by her magazine, Dorothy began hitting the bottle. She scraped by on translation work and freelance commissions, while her former contributors went on to bright and glittering careers of their own. Eventually, she left London for the more sedate charms of Cambridge – but she remained an inveterate flirt to the end. According to her grandson Olivier Todd, she had just convinced a young Italian woman to leave her husband for her shortly before she had to enter a clinic on account of her old age. She died at the age of 83.

ime magazine pronounced her "slender, durable News-hen Higgins".[38] But when it came to getting the story, *New York Herald Tribune* war reporter Marguerite "Maggie" Higgins (1920–1966) was more famed for her hard-nosed tenaciousness. When she had a baby, fellow *Herald Tribune* correspondent Homer Bigart reportedly said, "Wonderful, who's the mother?"[39] An Associated Press journalist once called her "the advance of women's lib."[40] (It was not meant as a compliment).

Maggie was born in Hong Kong in 1920, but her family moved back to the US when she was three years old. She went on to gain a BA in French at the University of California, Berkeley, and an MA at Columbia University School of Journalism. As a fresh-faced 22-year-old straight out of college, Maggie tricked her way past the receptionist and into the offices of the *Herald Tribune*, a now defunct but hugely respected New York newspaper, where she walked up to the city editor and asked for a job. She didn't get a spot at the time, but a sudden vacancy at the paper meant that she got one a year later. Maggie's father was a World War I airman, and she'd grown up reading the wartime novel *A Farewell to Arms*. "Despite Hemingway, or perhaps because of him, I have known since childhood that if there was to be a war I wanted to be there to know for myself what force cuts so deep in the hearts of men,"[41] Maggie recalled in her 1955 memoir *News Is a Singular Thing*.

Maggie had pleaded with her superiors for years to send her overseas; she got her wish with World War II. The newly minted war correspondent shipped out with the military in March 1945, just in time to see American soldiers liberate Germany. On 29 April, Maggie was one of the first two reporters to enter Dachau concentration camp. She and the troops of the US Seventh Army found 33,000 survivors, some so weak that they could only crawl toward their rescuers. "The mask of starvation was on all the

emaciated corpses," she filed in her despatch. "Many of the living were so frail it seemed impossible they could still be holding on to life."[42]

By 1947, Maggie's front page-making reports had made her Berlin bureau chief. Her success was marred, however, by rumours that she stole other reporters' stories, and that she would hop into bed with her sources if it meant securing an exclusive, even if actual proof of this was thin on the ground. "Reporters have to form a society of their own and behave as a society," *Herald Tribune* correspondent Stephen White sniffed in one letter. "Maggie treated all reporters as enemies, even the one or two she slept with to my knowledge."[43] The implication was clear: she wasn't a team player, and there was no room for her in the boys' club of foreign correspondents.

White also made a complaint about her alleged behaviour to her bosses in New York, and got her transferred to Tokyo in April 1950. This was, ironically, the making of Maggie's career. A month later, North Korean tanks steamrollered across the border with South Korea, catching the country and their American allies by surprise and catapulting the region into war. Unsurprisingly, Maggie was one of the first journalists on the plane to Seoul.

"For me, getting to Korea was more than just a story. It was a personal crusade," she said. "I could not let the fact that I was a woman jeopardize my newspaper's coverage of the war. Failure to reach the front would undermine all my arguments that I was entitled to the same assignment breaks as any man."[44]

There were another complications: *Tribune* war correspondent Homer Bigart had swanned into Korea and informed Maggie that she was to ship out to Tokyo or face a sacking, and he was followed closely by Lieutenant General Walton H Walker, who told her that he was throwing her out of Korea. Marguerite simply appealed to the commander-in-chief himself, General Douglas MacArthur. Once he lifted the ban, she proceeded to battle her way to the frontlines and stubbornly stayed there. One army lieutenant recalled seeing her immediately after he'd been grazed by a bullet: "I looked around and, oh, God!, there was Maggie Higgins. Every time you looked around, there she was!"[45] For her efforts, Maggie shared the 1951 Pulitzer Prize with Homer and four other Korean War journalists – she was the first woman to receive the award for foreign correspondence.

In 1963, Maggie flew out to Vietnam to cover the war and the recent spate of suicides by Buddhist monks. Two years into her assignment, she contracted what she initially thought to be dengue fever. It was leishmaniasis, a deadly tropical disease that attacks the kidneys and, in Maggie's case, proved resistant to treatment. She died at the age of 45 in a Washington, DC, army hospital. When asked for his opinion on his former rival, Homer grudgingly told one interviewer: "She was a very brave person, foolishly brave. As a result, I felt as though I had to go out and get shot at occasionally myself."[46]

INTRODUCTION

1 Woolf, Virginia. *A Room of One's Own*, Broadview Press, 2001, p.59.
2 Guest, Katy. "Male Writers Still Dominate Book Reviews and Critic Jobs, Vida Study Finds", *Guardian*, 19 Oct 2017. Accessed 5 March 2018. https://www.theguardian.com/books/booksblog/2017/oct/19/male-writers-still-dominate-book-reviews-and-critic-jobs-vida-study-finds
3 Underwood, Ted; Bamman, David; and Lee, Sabrina. "The Transformation of Gender in English-Language Fiction", *Cultural Analytics*, 13 Feb 2018. DOI: 10.22148/16.019. Accessed 4 Mar 2018. http://culturalanalytics.org/2018/02/the-transformation-of-gender-in-english-language-fiction/
4 Shamsie, Kamila. "Kamila Shamsie: Let's Have a Year of Publishing Only Women – a Provocation", *Guardian*, 5 June 2016. Accessed 4 March 2018. https://www.theguardian.com/books/2015/jun/05/kamila-shamsie-2018-year-publishing-women-no-new-books-men

POETS & PLAYWRIGHTS

1 Mendelson, Daniel. "Hearing Sappho", *New Yorker*, 12 Mar 2015. Accessed 20 Dec 2017. https://www.newyorker.com/books/page-turner/hearing-sappho
2 Sappho. *Sappho: A New Translation of the Complete Works*. Cambridge University Press, 2014, p.26.
3 Green, Peter. "What We Know", *London Review of Books*, vol. 37, no. 22 (19 Nov 2015). Accessed 20 Dec 2017. https://www.lrb.co.uk/v37/n22/peter-green/what-we-know
4 Ibid.
5 Sappho. *Sappho: A New Translation of the Complete Works*. Cambridge University Press, 2014, p.33.
6 Ibid., p.77.
7 Meador, Betty De Shong. "Sappho and Enheduanna". Presented at the conference "Ancient Greece/Modern Psyche", Sept 2009, p.2. Accessed 25 Jan 2018. http://www.zipang.org.uk/pdfs/Meador2009.pdf
8 Ibid., p.3. Accessed 25 Jan 2018. http://www.zipang.org.uk/pdfs/Meador2009.pdf
9 Douglas, Claire. "In Homage to the Feminine Self", *The San Francisco Jung Institute Library Journal*, vol. 21, no. 2 (2002), p.45. Accessed 30 Dec 2017. JSTOR, www.jstor.org/stable/pdf/10.1525/jung.1.2002.21.2.43.pdf?loggedin=true
10 Salisbury, Joyce E. *Encyclopedia of Women in the Ancient World*. ABC-CLIO, 2001, p.102.
11 Ostriker, Alicia. "Beyond Good and Evil", *The Women's Review of Books*, vol. 18, no. 10/11 (July 2001), p.37.
12 Salisbury, Joyce E. *Encyclopedia of Women in the Ancient World*. ABC-CLIO, 2001, p.101.
13 Lanyer, Aemilia. *Salve Deus Rex Judaeorum*, 1611. Accessed 22 Dec 2017. http://www.luminarium.org/renascence-editions/lanyer1.html
14 Bevington, David. "Rowse's Dark Lady" in Grossman, Marshall (ed.). *Aemilia Lanyer: Gender, Genre, and the Canon*. University Press of Kentucky, 13 Jan 2015, p.23.
15 Hudson, John. "Aemilia Lanyer", *Project Continua*. Accessed 22 Dec 2017. http://www.projectcontinua.org/aemilia-lanyer/#_edn7
16 Alvaraz, Julia. "Introduction", Grossman, Edith (trans.), and de la Cruz, Inez. *Sor Juana Inés de la Cruz: Selected Works*. W W Norton & Co., 2016.
17 de la Cruz, Juana. "Response of the Poet to the Very Eminent Sor Filotea de la Cruz" in Grossman, Edith (trans.), and de la Cruz, Inez. *Sor Juana Inés de la Cruz: Selected Works*. W W Norton & Co., 2016, p.160.
18 Ibid., p.173.
19 Accessed 23 Dec 2017. https://www.poetryfoundation.org/poets/sor-juana
20 de la Cruz, Juana. "Response of the Poet to the Very Eminent Sor Filotea de la Cruz" in Grossman, Edith (trans.), and de la Cruz, Inez. *Sor Juana Inés de la Cruz: Selected Works*. W W Norton & Co., 2016, p.71.
21 de la Cruz, Juana. "Redondilla 87" in Grossman, Edith (trans.), and de la Cruz, Inez. *Sor Juana Inés de la Cruz: Selected Works*. W W Norton & Co., 2016, p.28.
22 de la Cruz, Juana. "Response of the Poet to the Very Eminent Sor Filotea de la Cruz" in Grossman, Edith (trans.) and de la Cruz, Inez. *Sor Juana Inés de la Cruz: Selected Works*. W W Norton & Co., 2016, p.160.
23 Ibid., p.166.
24 Paz, Octavio. *Sor Juana or, the Traps of Faith*. The Belknap Press of Harvard University Press, 1988, p.465.
25 Berg, Daria. *Women and the Literary World in Early Modern China, 1580–1700*, p.147.
26 Frankel, Hans H. "Cai Yan and the Poems Attributed to Her", *Chinese Literature: Essays, Articles, Reviews*, vol. 5, no. 1/2, 1983, p.135. JSTOR, www.jstor.org/stable/495671
27 Ibid.
28 Ibid.
29 Ibid., p.136.
30 Ibid., p.155.
31 Stefanowska, A D, and Lee, Lily Xiao Hong (eds). *Biographical Dictionary of Chinese Women: Antiquity Through Sui, 1600 BCE–618 CE*. M E Sharpe, 2007, p.110.
32 Naravane, Vishwanath S. *Sarojini Naidu: An Introduction to Her Life, Work and Poetry*. Orient Blackswan
Private Ltd, 2012, p.18.
33 Ibid.
34 Ibid., p.58.
35 Ibid., p.59.
36 Ibid., p.61.
37 Ibid., p.30.
38 Ibid., p.34.
39 Ibid., p.128.
40 Ibid., p.72.
41 King, James. *Roland Penrose: The Life of a Surrealist*. Edinburgh University Press, 2016, p.47.
42 Accessed 28 Dec 2017. https://www.treadwells-london.com/event/valentine-penrose-surreal-occultress/
43 Chadwick, Whitney. *Women Artists and the Surrealist Movement*. Thames & Hudson, 1985, p.181.
44 Ibid.
45 Kaplan, Janet. "Review of Chadwick, Whitney. *Women Artists and the Surrealist Movement*", *Woman's Art Journal*, vol. 9, no. 2 (1988), p.47–49. JSTOR, www.jstor.org/stable/1358321
46 Bishop, Michael. "Women Poets of the Twentieth Century" in Stephens, Sonya (ed.). *A History of Women's Writing in France*. Cambridge University Press, 2000, p.211.
47 King, James. *Roland Penrose: The Life of a Surrealist*. Edinburgh University Press, 2016, p.49.
48 Ibid., p.87.
49 Marwood, Kimberley. "Imaginary Dimensions: Women, Surrealism and the Gothic" in Purves, Maria (ed.). *Women and Gothic*, p.51.
50 Ibid., p.49.
51 Moore, Marianne and Costello, Bonnie (eds). *The Selected Letters of Marianne Moore*. Penguin Classics, 1998, p.171.
52 Raphel, Adrienne. "The Marianne Moore Revival", *New Yorker*, 13 Apr 2016. Accessed 10 Jan 2018. https://www.newyorker.com/books/page-turner/the-marianne-moore-revival
53 Chiasson, Don. "All About My Mother", *New Yorker*, 11 Nov 2013. Accessed 10 Jan 2018. https://www.newyorker.com/magazine/2013/11/11/all-about-my-mother
54 Donald Hall. "Marianne Moore, The Art of Poetry No. 4", *Paris Review*, Issue 26, Summer–Fall 1961. Accessed 10 Jan 2018. https://www.theparisreview.org/interviews/4637/marianne-moore-the-art-of-poetry-no-4-marianne-moore
55 Ibid.
56 Moore, Marianne. "Picking and Choosing", *Observations: Poems*. Farrar, Straus and Giroux, 2016, p.51.
57 Moore, Marianne. "An Octopus", *Observations: Poems*. Farrar, Straus and Giroux, 2016, p.89.
58 Stokes, Emily. "Review of Linda Leavell, *Holding On Upside Down: The Life and Work of Marianne Moore*", *Guardian*, 22 Feb 2014. Accessed 11 Jan 2018. https://www.theguardian.com/books/2014/feb/22/holding-upside-down-marianne-moore-linda-leavell
59 "Leading Lady of US Verse", *Life*, 13 Jan 1967, p.37.
60 Ibid., p.42.
61 Ibid., p.40.
62 Sagawa, Chika, and Nakayasu,

Sawako. "Backside", *Poetry*, vol. 194, no. 1 (2009), p.6. Accessed 23 Dec 2017. JSTOR, www.jstor.org/stable/25706518

63 Sagawa, Chika. "Ocean Angel" in Nakayasu, Sawako (trans.). *The Collected Poems of Chika Sagawa*. Canarium Books, 2015, p.80.

64 Sagawa, Chika. "Diary" in Nakayasu, Sawako (trans.). *The Collected Poems of Chika Sagawa*. Canarium Books, 2015, p.135.

65 Nakayasu, Sawako (trans.). *The Collected Poems of Chika Sagawa*. Canarium Books, 2015, p.xv.

66 Beriozkina, Patricia, and Polivanov, Konstantin. *Anna Akhmatova and her Circle*. University of Arkansas Press, 1994, p.xxix.

67 Akhmatova, Anna. "When you're drunk it's so much fun", 1912. Accessed 23 Dec 2017. https://www.poetryfoundation.org/poets/anna-akhmatova

68 Akhmatova, Anna. "Remembrances" in Davies, Jessie. *Anna of All the Russias: The Life of Anna Akhmatova*. Lincoln Davies, 1988, p.26.

69 Akhmatova, Anna. "Pamiati 19 iiulia 1914", 1917. Accessed 23 Dec 2017. https://www.poetryfoundation.org/poets/anna-akhmatova

70 Akhmatova, Anna. "I'm not one of those who left their land", 1923. Accessed 23 Dec 2017. https://americanliterature.com/author/anna-akhmatova/poem/im-not-one-of-those-who-left-their-land

71 Beriozkina, Patricia and Polivanov, Konstantin. *Anna Akhmatova and her Circle*. University of Arkansas Press, 1994, p.lxiii–lxiv.

72 Davies, Jessie. *Anna of All the Russias: The Life of Anna Akhmatova*. Lincoln Davies, 1988, p.80.

73 Akhmatova, Anna. "Requiem 1935–1940", Davies, Jessie. *Anna of All the Russias: The Life of Anna Akhmatova*. Lincoln Davies, 1988, p.75.

74 Ascherson, Neal. "Our Lady of Sorrows", *Guardian*, 31 July 2005. Accessed 21 Dec. https://www.theguardian.com/books/2005/jul/31/biography.features

75 Jordan, June. *Soldier: A Poet's Childhood*. Basic Civitas Group, 2002. (Kindle Edition)

76 Accessed 18 Dec 2017. http://www.junejordan.net/about-june.html

77 Jordan, June. *Poem about Police Violence*. Accessed 18 Dec 2017. https://www.lambdaliterary.org/wp-content/uploads/2016/08/7.-June-Jordan.pdf

78 Jordan, June, *Soldier: A Poet's Childhood*. Basic Civitas Group, 2002. (Kindle Edition).

79 Accessed 18 Dec 2017. https://www.theguardian.com/news/2002/jun/20/guardianobituaries.booksobituaries

80 George, Lynell. "A Writer Intent on Rallying the Spirit of Survival", *Los Angeles Times*, 20 June 2002. Accessed 17 Dec 2017. http://articles.latimes.com/2002/jun/20/news/lv-jordan20

81 Jordan, June. "A New Politics of Sexuality", *Some of Us Did Not Die: New and Selected Essays of June Jordan*. Basic/Civitas Books, 2002

(Kindle Edition).

82 George, Lynell. "A Writer Intent on Rallying the Spirit of Survival", *Los Angeles Times*, 20 June 2002. Accessed 17 Dec 2017. http://articles.latimes.com/2002/jun/20/news/lv-jordan20

83 Jordan, June. "Introduction", *Some of Us Did Not Die: New and Selected Essays of June Jordan*. Basic/Civitas Books, 2002 (Kindle Edition).

84 Jordan, June, "Letter to R. Buckminster Fuller", *Some of Us Did Not Die: New and Selected Essays of June Jordan*. Basic/Civitas Books, 2002 (Kindle Edition).

85 Ibid.

86 Kuhn, Josh. "June Jordan by Josh Kuhn", *Bombe*, No. 55 (1 Oct 1995). Accessed 17 Dec 2017. https://bombmagazine.org/articles/june-jordan/

87 Ramírez, Dixa. *Dominicanas Presentes: Gender, Migration, and History's Legacy in Dominican Literature*. University of California, San Diego, 2011, p.52. Accessed 20 Dec 2017. https://escholarship.org/uc/item/85b060x5

88 Ramírez, Dixa. "Salomé Ureña's Blurred Edges: Race, Gender, and Commemoration in the Dominican Republic", *The Black Scholar*, vol. 45, no. 2 (2015), p.49. Accessed 20 Dec 2017. https://www.academia.edu/27955718/Salom%C3%A9_Ure%C3%B1as_Blurred_Edges_Race_Gender_and_Commemoration_in_the_Dominican_Republic

89 Ramírez, Dixa. *Dominicanas Presentes: Gender, Migration, and History's Legacy in Dominican Literature*. University of California, San Diego, 2011, p.68. Accessed 20 Dec 2017. https://escholarship.org/uc/item/85b060x5

90 Ramírez, Dixa. "Salomé Ureña's Blurred Edges: Race, Gender, and Commemoration in the Dominican Republic", *The Black Scholar*, vol. 45, no. 2 (2015), p.50. Accessed 20 Dec 2017. https://www.academia.edu/27955718/Salom%C3%A9_Ure%C3%B1as_Blurred_Edges_Race_Gender_and_Commemoration_in_the_Dominican_Republic

91 Hrotsvitha. *The Plays of Roswitha*. Translated by Christopher St. John, with an introduction by Cardinal Gasquet and a critical preface by the translator. Chatto & Windus, 1923. Accessed 17 Dec 2017. https://sourcebooks.fordham.edu/basis/roswitha-ros_pref.asp

92 Ibid.

93 Ibid.

94 Ibid.

95 Ibid.

96 Ibid.

97 H.D. *The Gift*, Virago Press, 1984, p.119.

98 "Imagism", *New World Encyclopedia*. Accessed 29 Dec 2017. http://www.newworldencyclopedia.org/entry/Imagism

99 Guest, Barbara. *Herself Defined: The Poet H.D. and Her World*. HarperCollins, 1985, p.9.

100 Ibid., p.23.

101 Ibid., p.24.

102 Ibid., p.24.

103 Ibid., p.7.

104 Ibid., p.43.

105 Doolittle, Hilda, *Collected Poems 1912–1944*. New Directions Publishing, 1986, p.174.

106 DuPlessis, Rachel Blau, and Friedman, Susan Stanford. "'Woman is Perfect': H.D.'s Debate with Freud", *Feminist Studies*, vol. 7, no. 3 (1981), p.425. JSTOR, www.jstor.org/stable/3177758

107 Doolittle, Hilda, *Collected Poems 1912–1944*. New Directions Publishing, 1986, p.519. Accessed 29 Dec 2017. https://www.poemhunter.com/hilda-doolittle/biography/

108 Ibid., p.613.

NOVELISTS & SHORT STORY WRITERS

1 Shikibu, Murasaki. *The Diary of Lady Murasaki*. Penguin Books Ltd, 1996. Kindle Location 1643.

2 Ibid., Kindle Locations 1270–1273.

3 Accessed 9 Dec 2017. https://onionandartichoke.wordpress.com/2015/12/01/who-is-tiptree-what-is-he/

4 Phillips, Julie. "Introduction: Who Is Tiptree, What Is He?", Phillips, Julie. *James Tiptree, Jr.: The Double Life of Alice B. Sheldon*. St. Martin's Press, 2006.

5 Ibid., p.78.

6 Ibid., p.142.

7 Ibid., p.248.

8 Ibid., p.257.

9 Ibid., p.361.

10 Enomoto, Yoshiko. "Breaking out of Despair: Higuchi Ichiyô and Charlotte Brontë", *Comparative Literature Studies* (1987), p 252. Accessed 4 Dec 2017. JSTOR, www.jstor.org/stable/pdf/40246384.pdf

11 Ibid.

12 Tanaka, Hisako. "Higuchi Ichiyo", *Monumenta Nipponica*, 1956, p.175.

13 Ibid., p.178.

14 Mitsutani, Margaret. "Higuchi Ichiyō: A Literature of Her Own", *Comparative Literature Studies*, vol. 22, no. 1 (1985), p.56.

15 Tanaka, Hisako. "Higuchi Ichiyo", *Monumenta Nipponica*, 1956, p.179.

16 Sarrazin, Albertine. *Astragal*. Serpent's Tail, 2014, p.23.

17 Ibid., p.51.

18 Ibid., p.160.

19 Smith, Patti. "Patti Smith: Why Albertine Sarrazin Is the Rebel Author I Can't Put Down", *New Statesman*, 20 Mar 2014. Accessed 10 Dec 2017. https://www.newstatesman.com/culture/2014/03/female-genet-albertine-sarrazin%E2%80%99s-astragal

20 Coppola, Carlo, and Zubair, Sajida. "Rashid Jahan: Urdu Literature's First Angry Young Woman", *Journal of South Asian Literature*, vol. 22, no. 1 (1987), p.166.

21 Accessed 13 Dec 2017. http://www.thehindu.com/features/metroplus/rebel-with-a-cause/article6201124.ece

22 Mirza, Begum Khurshid. *A Woman of Substance: The Memoirs of Begum Khurshid Mirza, 1918–1989*. Zubaan, 2005, p.100.

23 Ibid., p.94.

24 Accessed 13 Dec. https://urduwallahs.wordpress.com/2014/05/30/dili-ki-sair-story-by-

rasheed-jahan/
25 Coppola, Carlo, and Sajida Zubair. "Rashid Jahan: Urdu Literature's First Angry Young Woman", *Journal of South Asian Literature*, vol. 22, no. 1 (1987), p.170.
26 Ibid.
27 Accessed 13 Dec 2017. http://indianexpress.com/article/india/india-others/a-spark-that-lit-the-fire/
28 Ibid.
29 Choo, Christine. *Mission Girls: Aboriginal Women on Catholic Missions in the Kimberley, Western Australia, 1900–1950.* ISBS, 2001, p.164, Accessed 16 Dec 2017. https://www.findandconnect.gov.au/ref/wa/biogs/WE00023b.htm
30 Charles, Mary Carmel, and McGregor, William. *Winin: Why the Emu Cannot Fly.* Magabala Books, 1993. Accessed 16 Dec 2017. https://web.archive.org/web/20070828205513/http://magabala.com/authors/authatoh2.htm#a4
31 Ibid.
32 Cha, Theresa Hak Kyung. *Dictée.* University of California Press, 1982.
33 Accessed 11 Dec 2017. http://www.peeruk.org/template-3/
34 De Sousa, Bea, and Desgorgues, Juliette. *A Portrait in Fragments: Theresa Hak Kyung Cha 1951–1982.* Whitmont Press, 2013, p.22. Accessed 11 Dec. https://issuu.com/openshaw/docs/aportraitinfragments
35 Ibid., p.21.
36 Cha, Theresa Hak Kyung. *Dictée.* Third Woman Press, 1995, p.133.
37 Accessed 11 Dec 2017. http://www.robertatkins.net/beta/witness/artists/moves/tributes.html
38 Khalil-Habib, Nejmeh. *Samira Azzam (1926–1967): Memory of the Lost Land.* Accessed 10 Dec 2017. http://www.nobleworld.biz/images/samiraazam.pdf
39 Khalil-Habib, Nejmeh. "Al-Awda: the Theme of Return in Contemporary Arabic Literature: A Case-Study of Samira 'Azam", *Nebula* 5.5.2 (2008), p.92.
40 Khalil-Habib, Nejmeh. *Samira Azzam (1926–1967): Memory of the Lost Land.* Accessed 10 Dec 2017. http://www.nobleworld.biz/images/samiraazam.pdf
41 Suleiman, Yasir. "Palestine and the Palestinians in the Short Stories of Samīra 'Azzām", *Journal of Arabic Literature*, 1991, p.155.
42 Khalil-Habib, Nejmeh. "Al-Awda… A Case-Study of Samira 'Azam", *Nebula* 5.5.2 (2008), p.93.
43 Ibid., p.96.
44 Huang, Nicole. *Women, War, Domesticity: Shanghai Literature and Popular Culture of the 1940s.* Brill Academic Publishers, 2005, p.4.
45 Ibid., p.25.
46 Dooling, Amy. *Women's Literary Feminism in Twentieth-Century China.* Springer, 2005, p.158.
47 Ibid.
48 Ng, Janet. *The Experience of Modernity: Chinese Autobiography of the Early Twentieth Century.* University of Michigan Press, 2003, p.64.
49 Su Qing, "Waves", Silber, Cathy

(trans.), Dooling, Amy D, and Torgeson, Kristina M (eds). *Writing Women in Modern China: An Anthology of Women's Literature from the Early Twentieth Century.* Columbia University Press, 1998, pp.180–206.
50 Zarelli, Natalie. "One of the Earliest Science Fiction Books Was Written in the 1600s by a Duchess", *Atlas Obscura*, 16 Sept 2016. Accessed 6 Dec 2017. https://www.atlasobscura.com/articles/one-of-the-earliest-science-fiction-books-was-written-in-the-1600s-by-a-duchess
51 Accessed 6 Dec 2017. https://www.pepysdiary.com/diary/1667/04/11/
52 Whitaker, Katie. "Duchess of scandal", *Guardian*, 8 Aug 2013. Accessed 6 Dec 2017. https://www.theguardian.com/world/2003/aug/08/gender.uk
53 Accessed 6 Dec 2017. https://www.pepysdiary.com/diary/1667/04/11/
54 Accessed 6 Dec 2017. http://digital.library.upenn.edu/women/newcastle/blazing/blazing.html
55 Ibid.
56 Newcastle, Margaret Cavendish. *The Cavalier and his Lady: Selections from the Works of the First Duke and Duchess of Newcastle; edited with an introductory essay.* London Macmillan, 1872. Accessed 6 Dec 2017. https://archive.org/stream/cavalierandhis-la00newcuoft/cavalierandhisla00n-ewcuoft_djvu.txt
57 Zur Mühlen, Hermynia. *The End and the Beginning: The Book of My Life.* Open Book Publishers, 2010, p.20. Accessed 2 Dec 2017. http://books.openedition.org/obp/433
58 Ibid., p.19.
59 Ibid., p.23.
60 Ibid., p.156.
61 Gossman, Lionel. "Remembering Hermynia Zur Mühlen: A Tribute" in Zur Mühlen, Hermynia. *The End and the Beginning: The Book of My Life.* Open Book Publishers, 2010, p.272. Accessed 2 Dec 2017. http://books.openedition.org/obp/433
62 Ibid., p.23.
63 Ibid., p.156.
64 Françoise de Graffigny, "Correspondance de Madame de Graffigny", tome 11: 2 juillet 1750–19 juin 1751, *Lettres 1570–1722*, Dainard, J A (gen. ed.); with Curtis, J; Ducretet-Powell, M-P; Showalter, English and Smith, D W. Voltaire Foundation, 2007, p.365.
65 Ibid., p.94.
66 Showalter, English. "Graffigny at Cirey: A Fraud Exposed", *French Forum*, vol. 21, no. 1 (Jan 1996), p.29. Accessed 17 Dec 2017. JSTOR, www.jstor.org/stable/pdf/40551915.pdf
67 Françoise de Graffigny, "Correspondance de Madame de Graffigny", tome 11: 2 juillet 1750–19 juin 1751, *Lettres 1570–1722*, gen. ed. Dainard, J A (gen. ed.); Arthur, Dorothy P (ed.); with Curtis, J; Ducretet-Powell, M-P; Showalter, English and Smith, D W. Voltaire Foundation, 2007, p.586.
68 "Neshani Andreas: A Passion for Writing", The Free Library, 2004. *Sister Namibia.* Accessed 6 Dec 2017.

https://www.thefreelibrary.com/Neshani+Andreas%3a+a+passion+for+writing.-a0131994511
69 Ibid.
70 Ibid.
71 Ibid.
72 Andreas, Neshani. *The Purple Violet of Oshaantu.* Heinemann Educational Books, 2001, p.56.
73 "Neshani Andreas: A Passion for Writing", The Free Library. Accessed 6 Dec 2017. https://www.thefreelibrary.com/Neshani+Andreas%3a+a+passion+for+wriing.-a0131994511
74 Ibid.
75 Ibid.
76 Ibid.
77 Ibid.
78 "The Banned Book", *Hull Daily Mail*, 16 Nov 1928. Accessed 25 Nov 2017. https://blog.britishnewspaperarchive.co.uk/2013/11/15/the-obscenity-trial-of-miss-radclyffe-halls-novel-the-well-of-loneliness-16-november-1928/
79 Souhami, Diana. *The Trials of Radclyffe Hall.* Quercus, 2012, p.8.
80 Ibid., p.149.
81 Ibid., p.149.
82 Ibid., p.149.
83 Ibid., p.39.
84 Ibid., p.44.
85 Hall, Radclyffe, *The Well of Loneliness.* Jonathan Cape, 1928.
86 Ibid., p.195.
87 Troubridge, Una. *The Life and Death of Radclyffe Hall.* Hammond, 1961. Accessed 6 Nov 2017. https://ia600709.us.archive.org/9/items/TheLifeAndDeathOfRadclyffeHall corrected/0001.htm

HISTORIANS, ACADEMICS AND DIARISTS

1 Hillesum, Etty. *Etty: The Letters and Diaries of Etty Hillesum, 1941–1943.* Wm B Eerdmans Publishing, 2002, p.531.
2 Ibid., p.91.
3 Ibid., p.461.
4 Ibid., p.21.
5 Ibid., p.644.
6 Ibid., p.484.
7 Ibid., p.520.
8 Ibid., p.616.
9 Newman, Barbara. "Byzantine Laments", *London Review of Books*, vol. 39, no. 5 (2 March 2017). Accessed 31 Dec 2017. https://www.lrb.co.uk/v39/n05/barbara-newman/byzantine-laments
10 Komnene, Anna. *The Alexiad.* Frankopan, Peter (ed.) and Sewter, E R A (trans.). Penguin Books Ltd, 2009, p.515.
11 Ibid., p.496
12 Ibid., p.18.
13 Ibid., p.478.
14 Ibid., p.507
15 Ibid., p.513.
16 Quandahl, Ellen, and Jarratt, Susan C. "'To Recall Him…Will Be a Subject of Lamentation': Anna Comnena as Rhetorical Historiographer", *Rhetorica: A Journal of the History of Rhetoric*, vol. 26, no. 3 (2008), pp.301–35. JSTOR, www.jstor.org/stable/10.1525/rh.2008.26.3.301
17 Neville, Leonora. *Anna Komnene: The Life and Work of a Medieval Historian*, Oxford University Press,

2016, p.166.
18 Ibid.
19 Vassiltchikov, Marie 'Missie'. *The Berlin Diaries 1940–1945*. Pimlico, 1999, p.173.
20 Ibid., p.85.
21 Ibid., p.186.
22 Ibid., p.227.
23 Ibid., p.204.
24 Ibid., p.252.
25 Shōnagon, Sei. *The Pillow Book*. McKinney, Meredith (trans.). Penguin Books Ltd, 2005, p.256.
26 Shikibu, Murasaki. *The Diary of Lady Murasaki*. Bowring, Richard (trans.). Penguin Classics, 1996, p.54.
27 Ibid.
28 Shonagon, Sei. *The Pillow Book*. McKinney, Meredith (trans.). Penguin Books Ltd, 2005, p.26.
29 Ibid., p.25.
30 Ibid., p.55.
31 McKinney, Meredith. "What Is the Pillow Book?" in Shōnagon, Sei. *The Pillow Book*, Penguin Books Ltd. Kindle Edition, par. 5.
32 Shōnagon, Sei. *The Pillow Book*. McKinney, Meredith (trans.). Penguin Books Ltd, 2005, p.255.
33 Maria de Jesus, Carolina. *Child of the Dark: The Diary of Carolina Maria de Jesus*. Signet Classics, 2003, p.33.
34 Levine, Robert M. "The Cautionary Tale of Carolina Maria de Jesus", *Latin American Research Review*, vol. 29, no. 1 (1994), p.59.
35 Maria de Jesus, Carolina. *Child of the Dark: The Diary of Carolina Maria de Jesus*. Signet Classics, 2003, p.30.
36 St Clair, David. "Translator's Preface", in Maria de Jesus, Carolina. *Child of the Dark: The Diary of Carolina Maria de Jesus*. Signet Classics, 2003, p.xiii.
37 Ibid., p.xv.
38 Levine, Robert M. "The Cautionary Tale of Carolina Maria de Jesus", *Latin American Research Review*, vol. 29, no.1 (1994), p.64.
39 Maria de Jesus, Carolina. *Child of the Dark: The Diary of Carolina Maria de Jesus*. Signet Classics, 2003, p.34.
40 Fong, Grace S. "Writing self and writing lives: Shen Shanbao's (1808–1862) Gendered Auto/biographical Practices", *Nan Nü*, vol. 2, no. 2 (2000), p.297.
41 Ibid., p.299.
42 Ibid., p.275.
43 Ibid., p.265.
44 Ibid., p.293.
45 Ibid., p.294.
46 Ibid., p.295.
47 Elbe, Lili. *Man Into Woman: The First Sex Change, a Portrait of Lili Elbe: the True and Remarkable Transformation of the Painter Einar Wegener*. Blue Boat Books, 2004.
48 Ibid., p.259.
49 Ibid., p.61.
50 Ibid., p.61.
51 Ibid., p.62.
52 Ibid., p.66.
53 Ibid., p.94.
54 Ibid., p.100.
55 Ibid., p.260.
56 Ibid., p.266.

ESSAYISTS
1 http://classics.mit.edu/Euripides/andromache.html Accessed

29 Nov 2017.
2 Anger, Jane. *Jane Anger her Protection for Women*. London: Richard Jones and Thomas Orwin, 1589. Accessed 28 Nov 2017. http://digital.library.upenn.edu/women/anger/protection/protection.html
3 Ibid.
4 Ibid.
5 Ibid.
6 Ibid.
7 Hull, Gloria T. "Introduction" in Dunbar-Nelson, Alice Moore. *Give Us Each Day : The Diary of Alice Dunbar-Nelson*. W W Norton, 1984, p.20. Accessed 25 Nov 2017. https://archive.org/details/giveuseachday-di00dunb
8 Dunbar-Nelson, Alice Moore. "Brass Ankles Speaks", unpublished. Accessed 25 Nov 2017. http://www.english.illinois.edu/maps/poets/a_f/dunbar-nelson/essays.htm
9 Ibid.
10 Ibid.
11 Novak, Terry G. *Alice Dunbar-Nelson*. University of Minnesota, 2009. Accessed 25 Nov 2017. https://conservancy.umn.edu/bitstream/handle/11299/166289/Nelson%2C%20Alice%20Dunbar.pdf?sequence=1&isAllowed=y, p.2.
12 Hull, Gloria T. *Give Us Each Day: The Diary of Alice Dunbar-Nelson*, p.360. Accessed 25 Nov 2017. https://archive.org/stream/giveuseachday-00glor#page/20/mode/2up/search/husband
13 Ibid., p.197.
14 Ibid., p.303.
15 Ibid., p.383.
16 Ibid., p.393.
17 Hull, Gloria T. "Researching Alice Dunbar-Nelson: A Personal and Literary Perspective", *Feminist Studies*, vol. 6, no. 2 (1980), pp.314–20. JSTOR, www.jstor.org/stable/3177745, p.319.
18 Bacinetti Florenzi Waddington, Marianna. "Pantheism as the Foundation of the True and the Good" in Copenhaver, Brian P, and Copenhaver, Rebecca (eds). *From Kant to Croce: Modern Philosophy in Italy, 1800–1950*. University of Toronto Press, 2012, p.420.
19 Ibid.
20 Ghorayeb, Rose. "May Ziadeh (1886–1941)", *Signs: Journal of Women in Culture and Society*, vol. 5, no. 2 (1979), p.375.
21 Ibid.
22 Ibid., p.376.
23 Samman, Ghada, and Hassan, Fatme Sharafeddine (trans.). "The Victim of Beauty: Reviving the Literary Legacy of Mai Ziadeh", *Al Jadid*, vol. 5, no. 28 (Summer 1999). Accessed 1 Dec 2017. http://www.aljadid.com/content/victim-beauty-reviving-literary-legacy-mai-ziadeh
24 Accessed 1 Dec 2017. https://middleeastrevised.com/2014/10/30/remembering-may-ziadeh-ahead-of-her-time/
25 Samman, Ghada, and Hassan, Fatme Sharafeddine (trans). "The Victim Of Beauty: Reviving the Literary Legacy of Mai Ziadeh", *Al Jadid*, vol. 5, no. 28 (Summer 1999). Accessed 1 Dec 2017. http://www.

aljadid.com/content/victim-beauty-reviving-literary-legacy-mai-ziadeh
26 Accessed 26 Nov 2017. https://nzhistory.govt.nz/culture/maori-language-week/history-of-the-maori-language
27 Turia, Tariana and Sharples, Pita. "Passing of Dame Kāterina Te Heikōkō Mataira", *Scoop Media*, 16 July 2011. Accessed 26 Nov 2017. http://www.scoop.co.nz/stories/PA1107/S00302/passing-of-dame-katerina-te-heikoko-mataira.htm
28 Storylines. "Dame Kāterina Te Heikōkō Mataira", Storylines, no date listed. Accessed 26 Nov 2017. https://www.storylines.org.nz/Storylines+Profiles/Profiles+I-M/More+in+Profiles+I-M/Dame+Katerina+Te+Heikoko+Mataira.html
29 Millar, Nadine. "Poet and Politician: Sir Āpirana Ngata", *The Sapling*, 14 Sept 2017. Accessed 26 Nov 2017. https://www.thesapling.co.nz/single-post/2017/09/15/Poet-and-Politician-Sir-%C4%80pirana-Ngata
30 Turia, Tariana and Sharples, Pita. "Passing of Dame Kāterina Te Heikōkō Mataira", *Scoop Media*, 16 July 2011. Accessed 26 Nov 2017.
31 Hareven, Shulamith. "On Being a Levantine", *PN Review*, Manchester, vol. 18, no. 4 (1 Mar 1992), p.26. Accessed 1 Dec 2017. https://search.proquest.com/openview/6772b4d-6f022ce60130dcbe32964fe-b5/1?pq-origsite=gscholar&c-bl=1817849
32 Accessed 1 Dec 2017. http://www.nytimes.com/1992/03/17/books/writers-whose-fiction-stays-free-of-politics.html?pagewanted=all
33 Accessed 1 Dec. https://www.pnreview.org/encyclopedia/article/hareven-shulamith
34 Hareven, Shulamith. "On Being a Levantine", *PN Review*, Manchester, vol. 18, no. 4 (1 Mar 1992), p.26. Accessed 1 Dec 2017. https://search.proquest.com/openview/6772b4d-6f022ce60130dcbe32964fe-b5/1?pq-origsite=gscholar&c-bl=1817849
35 Farhi, Moris. "Shulamith Hareven: Voice of the Levant", *Jewish Quarterly*, vol. 38, no. 4 (1991), p.26. Accessed 1 Dec 2017. http://www.tandfonline.com/doi/abs/10.1080/0449010X.1991.10705815
36 Accessed 1 Dec 2017. https://jwa.org/encyclopedia/article/hareven-shulamith
37 Farhi, Moris, "Shulamith Hareven: Voice of the Levant", *Jewish Quarterly*, vol. 38, no. 4 (1991), p.26. Accessed 1 Dec 2017. http://www.tandfonline.com/doi/abs/10.1080/0449010X.1991.10705815
38 Chomsky, Noam. *Fateful Triangle: The United States, Israel, and the Palestinians*. South End Press, 1999, p.487.
39 Hertzberg, Arthur. "100 Years Later, a Jewish Writer's Time Has Come", *New York Times*, 31 Mar 1991. Accessed 1 Dec 2017. http://www.nytimes.com/1991/03/31/books/100-years-later-a-jewish-writer-s-time-has-come.html?pagewanted=all
40 Allen, Prudence, and Salvatore,

Filippo. "Lucrezia Marinelli and Woman's Identity in Late Italian Renaissance", *Renaissance and Reformation/Renaissance et Réforme*, 17 (1992). Accessed 3 Dec 2017. JSTOR, www.jstor.org/stable/43444859
41 Ibid., p.21.
42 Ibid., p.23.

JOURNALISTS AND EDITORS
1 *Truth*, 16 (11 Mar 1897), p.7. Cited in Linneman, William R. "Humorous Views of Yellow Journalism", *Studies in American Humor*, vol. 3, no. 1 (1976), p.25. JSTOR, www.jstor.org/stable/42573097
2 Bly, Nellie. "Chapter XIV: Some Unfortunate Stories", *Ten Days in a Mad-House*. Ian L Munroe, 1887. Accessed 6 Jan 2018. http://digital.library.upenn.edu/women/bly/madhouse/madhouse.html
3 Gay, Eva. "The Toiling Women", *St. Paul Globe*, 1 Apr 1888. Accessed 6 Jan 2018. http://dlib.nyu.edu/undercover/i-toiling-women-eva-gay-aka-eva-mcdonald-aka-eva-valesh-st-paul-globe
4 Ibid.
5 Quoted in Ammons, Elizabeth. "New Literary History: Edith Wharton and Jessie Redmon Fauset", *College Literature*, vol. 14, no. 3 (1987), p.215.
6 Quoted in Scutts, Joanna. "Absent Friends – Jessie Redmon Fauset", *Open Letters Monthly*, 1 Sept 2011. Accessed 6 Jan 2018. https://www.openlettersmonthly.com/oblivion/
7 Hughes, Langston. *"Big Sea": The Collected Works of Langston Hughes*. University of Missouri Press, 2001, p.173.
8 Fauset, Jessie Redmon. *The Chinaberry Tree: A Novel of American Life & Selected Writings*. UPNE, 1931. Cited in Walton, Anthony. "Double-Bind: Three Women of the Harlem Renaissance", Poets.org, 12 June 2007. Accessed 6 Jan 2018. https://www.poets.org/poetsorg/text/double-bind-three-women-harlem-renaissance
9 Fauset, Jessie Redmon. *Plum Bun*. Frederick A Stokes, 1928, p.241.
10 Hughes, Langston. *"Big Sea": Collected Works*. University of Missouri Press, 2001, p.192.
11 Quoted in Johnson, Abby Arthur. "Literary Midwife: Jessie Redmon Fauset and the Harlem Renaissance", *Phylon*, vol. 39, no. 2 (1978), p.147. JSTOR, www.jstor.org/stable/274509
12 Ibid., p.148.
13 Ibid., p.151.
14 Gurnay, Marie de. Preface of 1595, "Mais elle commença de désirer la connaissance, communication et bienveillance de leur Auteur plus que toutes les choses au monde" in Horowitz, Maryanne Cline (trans.). "Marie De Gournay, Editor of the *Essais* of Michel de Montaigne: A Case-Study in Mentor–Protegee Friendship", *The Sixteenth Century Journal*, vol. 17, no. 3 (1986), p.278. JSTOR, www.jstor.org/stable/2540321.
15 Montaigne, Michel de. *The Complete Essays of Montaigne*. Frame, Donald M (trans.). Stanford University Press, 1865, p.138. Quoted in Horowitz,

Maryanne Cline (trans.). "Marie De Gournay, Editor of the *Essais* of Michel de Montaigne: A Case-Study in Mentor–Protegee Friendship", *The Sixteenth Century Journal*, vol. 17, no. 3 (1986), p.278. JSTOR, www.jstor.org/stable/2540321
16 Ibid.
17 Dezon-Jones, Elyane. "Marie Le Jars de Gournay (1565–1645)". Sartori, Eva Martin, and Zimmerman, Dorothy Wynne (eds). *French Women Writers: A Bio-bibliographical Source Book*. Greenwood Publishing Group, 1991, p.201.
18 Schurman, Anna Maria van. *Opuscula*, p.264 (Leiden, 1648). Quoted in Larsen, Anne R. "A Women's Republic of Letters: Anna Maria Van Schurman, Marie De Gournay, and Female Self-Representation in Relation to the Public Sphere". *Early Modern Women*, vol. 3, 2008, pp.108. JSTOR, www.jstor.org/stable/23541520
19 Ibid.
20 Dezon-Jones, Elyane. "Marie Le Jars de Gournay (1565–1645)". Sartori, Eva Martin, and Zimmerman, Dorothy Wynne (eds). *French Women Writers: A Bio-bibliographical Source Book*. Greenwood Publishing Group, 1991, p.203.
21 Jabavu, N. "Smuts and I", *Daily Dispatch*, 9 Feb 1977. Quoted in Xaba, Makhosazana. "Noni Jabavu: A Peripatetic Writer Ahead of Her Times", *Tydskrif vir Letterkunde*, vol. 46, no. 1 (2009). Accessed 7 Jan 2018. http://www.scielo.org.za/scielo.php?script=sci_arttext&pid=S0041-476X2009000100017
22 Ibid.
23 Jabavu, N. *Drawn in Colour: African Contrasts*. John Murray, 1960, p.ix.
24 Ibid., p.ix.
25 Ibid., p.149.
26 Accessed 7 Jan 2018. https://www.kirkusreviews.com/book-reviews/noni-jabavu/drawn-in-color/
27 Ibid.
28 Jabavu, N. *Drawn in Color: African Contrasts*. John Murray, 1960, p.13.
29 Ibid.
30 Javabu, N. "From the Editor Abroad", *The New Strand*, Feb 1962. Quoted in Xaba, Makhosazana. "Noni Jabavu: A Peripatetic Writer Ahead of Her Times", *Tydskrif vir Letterkunde*, vol. 46, no. 1 (2009). Accessed 7 Jan 2018. http://www.scielo.org.za/scielo.php?script=sci_arttext&pid=S0041-476X2009000100017
31 Accessed 7 Jan 2018. http://www.sahistory.org.za/people/helen-nontando-noni-jabavu
32 Kavanagh, Julie. *Secret Muses: The Life of Frederick Ashton*. Faber & Faber, 1996, p.73. Cited in Carrod, Amanda Juliet. "A Plea for a Renaissance: Dorothy Todd's Modernist Experiment in British Vogue, 1922–1926". Diss. Keele University, 2015, p.216.
33 Anonymous. "Contents Page", *Vogue*, early Apr 1926, p.xiv. Cited in Carrod, Amanda Juliet. "A Plea for a Renaissance: Dorothy Todd's Modernist Experiment in British Vogue, 1922–1926". Diss. Keele University, 2015, p.97.

34 Mortimer, Raymond. "The Fashions of the Mind", *Vogue*, early Feb 1924, p.49. Cited in Carrod, Amanda Juliet. "A Plea for a Renaissance: Dorothy Todd's Modernist Experiment in British Vogue, 1922–1926". Diss. Keele University, 2015, p.6.
35 Huxley, Aldous. Cited in Kavanagh, Julie. *Secret Muses: The Life of Frederick Ashton*, Faber & Faber, 1996, p.74. Cited in Carrod, Amanda Juliet. "A Plea for a Renaissance: Dorothy Todd's Modernist Experiment in British Vogue, 1922–1926". Diss. Keele University, 2015, p.214.
36 Editorial, *Vogue*, early Nov 1925, p. xlvii. Cited in Reed, Christopher. "Design for (Queer) Living: Sexual Identity, Performance, and Decor in British Vogue, 1922–1926." *GLQ: A Journal of Lesbian and Gay Studies*, vol. 12, no. 3 (2006), p.379.
37 Vita Sackville-West in a letter to Harold Nicholson dated 24 Sept 1926. Cited in Carrod, Amanda Juliet. "A Plea for a Renaissance: Dorothy Todd's Modernist Experiment in British Vogue, 1922–1926". Diss. Keele University, 2015, p.240.
38 "Pride of the Regiment", *Time*, 25 Sept 1950, p.63–64. Quoted in Murray, Peter Noel. "Marguerite Higgins: An Examination of Legacy and Gender Bias". Diss. University of Maryland, 2003, p.24.
39 Salisbury, Harrison E. "Introduction" in Bigart, Homer. *Forward Positions: The War Correspondence of Homer Bigart*. University of Arkansas Press, 1992, p.xxiii.
40 Keeshen, Kathleen Kearney. "Marguerite Higgins: Journalist, 1920–1966", Ph.D diss. University of Maryland, 1983, p.140.
41 Higgins, Marguerite. *News is a Singular Thing*. Doubleday, 1955, p.30.
42 Higgins, Marguerite. "33,000 Dachau Captives Freed by 7th Army", *New York Herald Tribune*, 1 May 1945, quoted in Sofsky, Wolfgang. *The Order of Terror: The Concentration Camp*. Princeton University Press, 2013.
43 White, Stephen. "Letter to Richard Kluger", 15 Oct 1981, Box 16, Folder 348, Richard Kluger Papers. Manuscripts and Archives, Yale University Library.
44 Higgins, Marguerite. *War in Korea*. Doubleday & Co., 1951, p.17.
45 Knox, Donald, *The Korean War: Pusan to Chosin: An Oral History*. Harvest Books, 2002, p.279.
46 Pride, Mike. "The Jury Has Spoken", *Columbia Journalism Review*, Spring 2016. Accessed 1 Jan 2018. https://www.cjr.org/the_feature/the_jury_has_spoken.php

POETS & PLAYWRIGHTS
Sappho
Beard, Mary. "Sappho Speaks", *London Review of Books*, vol. 12, no. 19 (11 Oct 1990). Accessed 20 Dec 2017. https://www.lrb.co.uk/v12/n19/mary-beard/sappho-speaks
Green, Peter. "What We Know", *London Review of Books*, vol. 37, no. 22 (19 Nov 2015). Accessed 20 Dec 2017. https://www.lrb.co.uk/v37/n22/peter-green/what-we-know
Hall, Edith. "Sensual Sappho", *New York Review of Books*, 7 May 2015. Accessed 20 Dec 2017. http://www.nybooks.com/articles/2015/05/07/sensual-sappho/
Mendelsohn, Daniel. "Girl, Interrupted", *New Yorker*, 16 Mar 2015. Accessed 20 Dec 2017. https://www.newyorker.com/magazine/2015/03/16/girl-interrupted
Mendelson, Daniel. "Hearing Sappho", *New Yorker*, 12 Mar 2015. Accessed 20 Dec 2017. https://www.newyorker.com/books/page-turner/hearing-sappho
Sappho. *Sappho: A New Translation of the Complete Works*. Cambridge University Press, 2014.

Enheduanna
Douglas, Claire. "In Homage to the Feminine Self", *The San Francisco Jung Institute Library Journal*, vol. 21, no. 2 (2002), p 43–58. Accessed 30 Dec 2017. JSTOR, www.jstor.org/stable/pdf/10.1525/jung.1.2002.21.2.43.pdf?loggedin=true
Hafford, Brad. "Ur Digitization Project: Item of the Month, June 2012". Penn Museum. Accessed 30 Dec 2017. https://www.penn.museum/blog/museum/ur-digitization-project-item-of-the-month-june-2012/
Mark, Joshua J. "Enheduanna", *Ancient History Encyclopedia*. Last modified 24 Mar 2014. Accessed 30 Dec 2017. https://www.ancient.eu/Enheduanna/
Meador, Betty De Shong. *Inanna, Lady of Largest Heart: Poems of the Sumerian High Priestess Enheduanna*. University of Texas Press, 2000.
Meador, Betty De Shong. "Sappho and Enheduanna". Presented at the conference "Ancient Greece/Modern Psyche", Sept 2009. Accessed 25 Jan 2018. http://www.zipang.

org.uk/pdfs/Meador2009.pdf
Ostriker, Alicia. "Beyond Good and Evil", *The Women's Review of Books*, vol. 18, no. 10/11 (July 2001).
Salisbury, Joyce E. *Encyclopedia of Women in the Ancient World*. ABC-CLIO, 2001.
Smith, Bonnie G. *The Oxford Encyclopedia of Women in World History*, vol. 1. New York: Oxford University Press, Inc., 2008.
Wayne, Tiffany K (ed.). *Feminist Writings from Ancient Times to the Modern World: A Global Sourcebook and History*. ABC-CLIO, 2011.

Aemilia Lanyer
Bevington, David. "Rowse's Dark Lady", in Grossman, Marshall (ed). *Aemilia Lanyer: Gender, Genre, and the Canon*. University Press of Kentucky, 13 Jan 2015.
Chedgzoy, Kate. "Remembering Aemilia Lanyer", *Journal of the Northern Renaissance*, vol. 2, 2010. Accessed 21 Dec 2017. http://www.northernrenaissance.org/remembering-aemilia-lanyer/
Hudson, John. "Aemilia Lanyer", *Project Continua*. Accessed 22 Dec 2017. http://www.projectcontinua.org/aemilia-lanyer/#_edn7
Lanyer, Aemilia. *Salve Deus Rex Judaeorum*, 1611. Accessed 22 Dec 2017. http://www.luminarium.org/renascence-editions/lanyer1.html
Simon, Ed. "Amelia Lanyer, the First Female Jewish English Poet and Shakespeare's Dark Lady?" *Tablet*, 22 Apr 2016. Accessed 21 Dec 2017. http://www.tabletmag.com/jewish-arts-and-culture/books/200521/amelia-lanyer-english-poet
Simonds, Sandra. "On Shakespeare and Aemilia Lanyer", *Granta*, 19 Apr 2016. Accessed 21 Dec 2017. https://granta.com/shakespeare-aemilia-lanyer/
Accessed 21 Dec 2017. https://www.bl.uk/collection-items/emilia-laniers-salve-deus-rex-judaeorum-1611
Accessed 21 Dec 2017. http://britrenpoetry.wikidot.com/aemilia-lanyer
Accessed 21 Dec 2017. https://www.poetryfoundation.org/poets/aemilia-lanyer

Sor Juana Inés de la Cruz
Alvaraz, Julia. "Introduction" in Grossman, Edith (trans.), and de la Cruz, Inez. *Sor Juana Inés de la Cruz: Selected Works*. W W Norton & Co., 2016.
Baker, Katie. "Sor Juana: Mexico's Most Erotic Poet and Its Most Dangerous Nun", *The Daily Beast*, 11 Aug 2014. Accessed 23 Dec 2017. https://www.thedailybeast.com/sor-juana-mexicos-most-erotic-poet-and-its-most-dangerous-nun
Grossman, Edith (trans.), and de la Cruz, Inez. *Sor Juana Inés de la Cruz: Selected Works*. W W Norton & Co., 2016.
Grossman-Heinze, Dahlia. "My Favorite Feminist: Sor Juana Inés de la Cruz", *Ms Magazine*,

16 Mar 2011. Accessed 23 Dec 2017. http://msmagazine.com/blog/2011/03/16/my-favorite-feminist-sor-juana-ines-de-la-cruz/
Paz, Octavio. *Sor Juana or, the Traps of Faith*. The Belknap Press of Harvard University Press, 1988.
Villela, Khristaan D. "The Tenth Muse of Mexico: Sor Juana Inés de la Cruz", *Pasatiempo*, 16 Oct 2015. Accessed 23 Dec 2017. www.santafenewmexican.com/pasatiempo/books/the-tenth-muse-of-mexico-sor-juana-in-s-de/article_1f5e16a5-6a1e-510c-a686-44f70f77a281.html
Yugar, Theresa A. *Sor Juana Ines de la Cruz: Feminist Reconstruction of Biography and Text*. Wipf and Stock Publishers, 2014.
Accessed 23 Dec 2017. https://www.poetryfoundation.org/poets/sor-juana

Cai Yan
Berg, Daria. *Women and the Literary World in Early Modern China, 1580–1700*. Routledge, 2015.
Chang, Kang-I; Sun, Haun Saussy; and Yim-tze Kwong, Charles. *Women Writers of Traditional China: An Anthology of Poetry and Criticism*. Stanford University Press, 1999.
Chang, Taiping, and Knechtges, David R. (eds). *Ancient and Early Medieval Chinese Literature: A Reference Guide*. Brill, 2010.
Frankel, Hans H. "Cai Yan and the Poems Attributed to Her", *Chinese Literature: Essays, Articles, Reviews*, vol. 5, no. 1/2, 1983. JSTOR, www.jstor.org/stable/495671
Rouzer, Paul F. *Articulated Ladies: Gender and the Male Community in Early Chinese Texts*. Harvard University Asia Center, 2001.
Stefanowska, A D, and Lee, Lily Xiao Hong (eds). *Biographical Dictionary of Chinese Women: Antiquity Through Sui, 1600 BCE–618 CE*. M E Sharpe, 2007.

Sarojini Naidu
Nair, Karthika S. "Sarojini Naidu: The Nightingale of India | #IndianWomenInHistory", *Feminism in India*, 22 Mar 2017. Accessed 21 Dec 2017. com/2017/03/22/sarojini-naidu-essay/
Naravane, Vishwanath S. *Sarojini Naidu: An Introduction to Her Life, Work and Poetry*. Orient Blackswan Private Ltd, 2012.
Ray, Sanjana. "Celebrating the Legacy of Sarojini Naidu, the Driving Force Behind Women's Equality in India", *YourStory*, Feb 2017. Accessed 21 Dec 2017. com/2017/02/celebrating-legacy-sarojini-naidu-driving-force-behind-womens-equality-india/

Valentine Penrose
Bishop, Michael. "Women Poets of the Twentieth Century" in Stephens, Sonya (ed.). *A History of Women's Writing in France*. Cambridge University Press, 2000.
Chadwick, Whitney. *The Militant*

Muse: Love, War and the Women of Surrealism. Thames & Hudson, 2017.

Chadwick, Whitney. *Women Artists and the Surrealist Movement*. Thames & Hudson, 1985.

Hubert, R R. *Magnifying Mirrors: Women, Surrealism, & Partnership*. University of Nebraska Press, 1994.

Kaplan, Janet. "Review of Chadwick, Whitney. *Women Artists and the Surrealist Movement*", *Woman's Art Journal*, vol. 9, no. 2 (1988), pp. 47–49. JSTOR, www.jstor.org/stable/1358321

King, James. *Roland Penrose: The Life of a Surrealist*. Edinburgh University Press, 2016.

Marwood, Kimberley. "Imaginary Dimensions: Women, Surrealism and the Gothic" in Purves, Maria (ed.). *Women and Gothic*. Cambridge Scholars Publishing, 2014. Accessed 28 Dec 2017. https://www.treadwells-london.com/event/valentine-penrose-surreal-occultress/

Marianne Moore

Chiasson, Don. "All About My Mother", *New Yorker*, 11 Nov 2013. Accessed 10 Jan 2018. https://www.newyorker.com/magazine/2013/11/11/all-about-my-mother

Hall, Donald. "Marianne Moore, The Art of Poetry No. 4", *Paris Review*, Issue 26, Summer–Fall 1961. Accessed 10 Jan 2018. https://www.theparisreview.org/interviews/4637/marianne-moore-the-art-of-poetry-no-4-marianne-moore

Logenbach, James. "Less is Moore", *The Nation*, 31 Mar 2016. Accessed 10 Jan 2018. https://www.thenation.com/article/less-is-moore/

Moore, Marianne. *Observations: Poems*. Farrar, Straus and Giroux, 2016.

Moore, Marianne and Costello, Bonnie (eds). *The Selected Letters of Marianne Moore*. Penguin Classics, 1998.

Raphel, Adrienne. "The Marianne Moore Revival", *New Yorker*, 13 Apr 2016. Accessed 10 Jan 2018. https://www.newyorker.com/books/page-turner/the-marianne-moore-revival

Stokes, Emily. "Review of Linda Leavell, *Holding On Upside Down: The Life and Work of Marianne Moore* ", *Guardian*, 22 Feb 2014. Accessed 11 Jan 2018. https://www.theguardian.com/books/2014/feb/22/holding-upside-down-marianne-moore-linda-leavell

Whitman, Alden. "Shaper of Subtle Images", *New York Times*, 6 Feb 1972. Accessed 10 Jan 2018. http://www.nytimes.com/1972/02/06/archives/shaper-of-subtle-images.html

"Marianne Moore, 1887–1972". Poetry Foundation. Accessed 10 Jan 2018. https://www.poetryfoundation.org/poets/marianne-moore

"Leading Lady of US Verse", *Life*, 13 Jan 1967.

Sagawa Chika

Nagai, Mariko. "Remembering the Forgotten Woman of Japanese Modernism", *Japan Times*, 12 Nov 2016. Accessed 23 Dec 2017. https://www.japantimes.co.jp/culture/2016/11/12/books/book-reviews/remembering-forgotten-woman-japanese-modernism/#.Wj5XSlSFiRs

Nakayasu, Sawako (trans.). *The Collected Poems of Chika Sagawa*. Canarium Books, 2015.

Raphel, Adrienne. "The Startling Poetry of a Nearly Forgotten Japanese Modernist", *New Yorker*, 18 Aug 2015. Accessed 23 Dec 2017. https://www.newyorker.com/books/page-turner/the-startling-poetry-of-a-nearly-forgotten-japanese-modernist

Sagawa, Chika, and Nakayasu, Sawako. "Backside", *Poetry*, vol. 194, no. 1 (2009), p.6. JSTOR, Accessed 23 Dec 2017. www.jstor.org/stable/25706518

Anna Akhmatova

Akhmatova, Anna. "I'm not one of those who left their land", 1923. Accessed 23 Dec 2017. https://americanliterature.com/author/anna-akhmatova/poem/im-not-one-of-those-who-left-their-land

Akhmatova, Anna. "Pamiati 19 iiulia 1914", 1917. Accessed 23 Dec 2017. https://www.poetryfoundation.org/poets/anna-akhmatova

Akhmatova, Anna. "When you're drunk it's so much fun", 1912. Accessed 23 Dec 2017. https://www.poetryfoundation.org/poets/anna-akhmatova

Ascherson, Neal. "Our Lady of Sorrows", the *Guardian*, 31 July 2005. Accessed 21 Dec. https://www.theguardian.com/books/2005/jul/31/biography.features

Beriozkina, Patricia, and Polivanov, Konstantin. *Anna Akhmatova and her Circle*. University of Arkansas Press, 1994.

Davies, Jessie. *Anna of All the Russias: The Life of Anna Akhmatova*. Lincoln Davies, 1988.

Grushin, Olga. "Not Silenced", *New York Times*, 19 Mar 2006. Accessed 23 Dec 2017. http://www.nytimes.com/2006/03/19/books/review/not-silenced.html

Accessed 23 Dec 2017. http://www.poetrymagazines.org.uk/magazine/record.asp?id=5714

Accessed 23 Dec 2017. https://www.poetryfoundation.org/poets/anna-akhmatova#tab-poems

June Jordan

Busby, Margaret. "June Jordan." the *Guardian*, 20 June 2002. Accessed 17 Dec 2017. https://www.theguardian.com/news/2002/jun/20/guardianobituaries.booksobituaries

George, Lynell. "A Writer Intent on Rallying the Spirit of Survival", *Los Angeles Times*, 20 June 2002. Accessed 17 Dec 2017. http://

articles.latimes.com/2002/jun/20/news/lv-jordan20

Jordan, June. *Poem about Police Violence*. Accessed 18 Dec 2017. https://www.lambdaliterary.org/wp-content/uploads/2016/08/7.-June-Jordan.pdf

Jordan, June. *Soldier: A Poet's Childhood*. Basic Civitas Group, 2002 (Kindle Edition).

Jordan, June. *Some of Us Did Not Die: New and Selected Essays of June Jordan*. Basic/Civitas Books, 2002 (Kindle Edition).

Kinlock, Valerie. *June Jordan: Her Life and Letters*. Greenwood Publishing Group, 2006.

Kuhn, Josh. "June Jordan by Josh Kuhn", *Bombe*, No. 55 (1 Oct 1995). Accessed 17 Dec 2017. https://bombmagazine.org/articles/june-jordan/

St Felix, Doreen. "Out of Print: June Jordan", *Lenny Letter*, 30 Sept 2015. Accessed 17 Dec 2017. http://www.elle.com/culture/books/a30733/out-of-print-june-jordan/

Smith, Dinitia. "June Jordan, 65, Poet and Political Activist", *New York Times*, 18 June 2002. Accessed 17 Dec 2017. http://www.nytimes.com/2002/06/18/arts/june-jordan-65-poet-and-political-activist.html Accessed 17 Dec 2017. https://www.poetryfoundation.org/poets/june-jordan

Accessed 18 Dec 2017. https://www.theguardian.com/news/2002/jun/20/guardianobituaries.booksobituaries

Salomé Ureña

André, María Claudia, and Bueno, Eva Paulino Bueno (eds). *Latin American Women Writers: An Encyclopedia*. Routledge, 2014.

Marting, Diane E. (ed.). *Spanish American Women Writers: A Bio-bibliographical source book*. Greenwood Publishing Group, 1990.

Ramírez, Dixa. *Dominicanas Presentes: Gender, Migration, and History's Legacy in Dominican Literature*. University of California, San Diego, 2011. Accessed 20 Dec 2017. https://escholarship.org/uc/item/85b060x5

Ramírez, Dixa. "Salomé Ureña's Blurred Edges: Race, Gender, and Commemoration in the Dominican Republic", *The Black Scholar*, vol. 45, no. 2 (2015). Accessed 20 Dec 2017. https://www.academia.edu/27955718/Salom%C3%A9_Ure%C3%B1as_Blurred_Edges_Race_Gender_and_Commemoration_in_the_Dominican_Republic

Hrotsvitha of Gandersheim

Brown, Phyllis R, and Wailes, Stephen L (eds). *A Companion to Hrotsvit of Gandersheim (fl. 960): Contextual and Interpretive Approaches*. Brill, 2012.

Brown, Phyllis Rugg; Wilson, Katharina M; and McMillin, Linda A (eds). *Hrotsvit of Gandersheim: Contexts, Identities, Affinities, and Performances*. University of Toronto Press, 2004.

Hrotsvitha. *The Plays of Roswitha*. Translated by Christopher St. John, with an introduction by Cardinal Gasquet and a critical preface by the translator. Chatto & Windus, 1923. Accessed 17 Dec 2017. https://sourcebooks.fordham.edu/basis/roswitha-ros_pref.asp
Hudson, William Henry. "Hrotsvitha of Gandersheim", *The English Historical Review*, vol. 3, no. 11 (1888), pp.431–57. JSTOR, www.jstor.org/stable/546611
Lepine, Kristen. "Hrotsvit: 'Strong Voice of Medieval Literature'", *Historic Heroines*, 26 July 2016. Accessed 17 Dec 2017. http://historicheroines.org/2016/07/26/hrotsvit-strong-voice-medieval-literature/
Newlands, Carole E. "Hrotswitha's Debt to Terence", *Transactions of the American Philological Association*, vol. 116, 1986, pp.369–91. JSTOR, www.jstor.org/stable/283926
Wilson, Katharina M. *Hrotsvit of Gandersheim: A Florilegium of her Works*. Boydell & Brewer, 1998.

H.D.
DuPlessis, Rachel Blau, and Friedman, Susan Stanford. "'Woman is Perfect': H.D.'s Debate with Freud", *Feminist Studies*, vol. 7, no. 3 (1981), pp.417–30. JSTOR, www.jstor.org/stable/3177758
Guest, Barbara. *Herself Defined: The Poet H.D. and Her World*. HarperCollins, 1985.
H.D. *The Gift*, Virago Press, 1984.
Hernandez, H. "A Brief Biography of H.D", Imagists.org, 27 June 2015. Accessed 29 Dec 2017. http://www.imagists.org/hd/bio.html
Madrid, Anthony. "H.D. Notebook", *The Paris Review*, 3 May 2017. Accessed 29 Dec 2017. https://www.theparisreview.org/blog/2017/05/03/h-d-notebook/
Mandel, Charlotte. "Letters Across the Atlantic: H.D., Bryher, May Sarton, during World War II", Imagists. org, 27 Dec 2001. Accessed 29 Dec 2017. http://www.imagists.org/hd/hdcmone.html
Mills, Billy. "HD in London: When Imagism arrived" the *Guardian*, 5 May 2011. Accessed 29 Dec 2017 https://www.theguardian.com/books/booksblog/2011/may/05/hd-london-imagism
Accessed 29 Dec 2017. https://www.poetryfoundation.org/poets/h-d
Accessed 29 Dec 2017. https://www.poemhunter.com/hilda-doolittle/biography/
Accessed 29 Dec 2017. http://www.newworldencyclopedia.org/entry/Imagism

NOVELISTS & SHORT STORY WRITERS
Murasaki Shikibu
Buruma, Ian. "The Sensualist", *New Yorker*, 20 July 2015. Accessed 11 Dec 2017. http://www.newyorker.com/magazine/2015/07/20/the-sensualist-books-buruma

Shikibu, Murasaki. *The Diary of Lady Murasaki*. Penguin Books Ltd, 1996.
Tyler, Royall. "Murasaki Shikibu", *Harvard Magazine*, May–June 2002. Accessed 11 Dec 2017. http://www.harvardmagazine.com/2002/05/murasaki-shikibu.html

James Tiptree Jr.
Phillips, Julie. *James Tiptree, Jr.: The Double Life of Alice B. Sheldon*. St. Martin's Press, 2006. Accessed 9 Dec 2017. https://onionandartichoke.wordpress.com/2015/12/01/who-is-tiptree-what-is-he

Higuchi Ichiyō
Enomoto, Yoshiko. "Breaking out of Despair: Higuchi Ichiyō and Charlotte Brontë", *Comparative Literature Studies* (1987), pp.251–63. Accessed 4 Dec 2017. JSTOR, www.jstor.org/stable/pdf/40246384.pdf
Mitsutani, Margaret. "Higuchi Ichiyō: A Literature of Her Own", *Comparative Literature Studies*, vol. 22, no. 1 (1985).
Tanaka, Shaun. "Higuchi Ichiyo", *Monumenta Nipponica*, 1956. Accessed 4 Dec 2017. https://www.tofugu.com/japan/higuchi-ichiyo/

Albertine Sarrazin
Jordan, Laura. "The Rebellious Artistry of Albertine Sarrazin", *AnOther*. Accessed 10 Dec 2017. http://www.anothermag.com/fashion-beauty/7858/the-rebellious-artistry-of-albertine-sarrazin
Lanser, Susan. "Books Abroad", *Books Abroad*, vol. 49, no. 4 (1975), p.724. JSTOR, www.jstor.org/stable/40129799
Monson-Rosen, Madeleine. *Astragal by Albertine Sarrazin*, Patsy Southgate (trans.) on Bookslut. Accessed 10 Dec 2017. http://www.bookslut.com/fiction/2013_06_020126.php
Motte, Warren F Jr. "Albertine Sarrazin (1937–1967)", in Sartori, Eva Martin, and Zimmerman, Dorothy Wynne (eds). *French Women Writers*, University of Nebraska Press, 1994, pp.423–29.
Sarrazin, Albertine. *Astragal*. Serpent's Tail, 2014.
Smith, Patti. "Patti Smith: Why Albertine Sarrazin Is the Rebel Author I Can't Put Down", *New Statesman*, 30 Mar 2014. Accessed 10 Dec 2017. https://www.newstatesman.com/culture/2014/03/female-genet-albertine-sarrazin%E2%80%99s-astragal
Tompkins, Jeff. "Her Life to Live: Albertine Sarrazin's 'Astragal'", *Popmatters*. Accessed 10 Dec 2017. https://www.popmatters.com/172907-astragal-by-albertine-sarrazin-2495745501.html

Rashid Jahan
Coppola, Carlo, and Zubair, Sajida. "Rashid Jahan: Urdu Literature's First Angry Young Woman", *Journal of South Asian Literature*, vol. 22,

no. 1 (1987).
Mirza, Begum Khurshid. *A Woman of Substance: The Memoirs of Begum Khurshid Mirza, 1918–1989*. Zubaan, 2005. Accessed 13 Dec 2017. https://www.asymptotejournal.com/criticism/a-rebel-and-her-cause-the-life-and-work-of-rashid-jahan/
Accessed 13 Dec 2017. https://scroll.in/article/666833/why-fundamentalists-got-this-urdu-book-banned-in-1933
Accessed 13 Dec 2017. http://www.thehindu.com/features/metroplus/rebel-with-a-cause/article6201124.ece
Accessed 13 Dec. https://urduwallahs.wordpress.com/2014/05/30/dili-ki-sair-story-by-rasheed-jahan/
Accessed 13 Dec 2017. http://indianexpress.com/article/india/india-others/a-spark-that-lit-the-fire/

Mary Carmel Charles
Charles, Mary Carmel, and McGregor, William. *Winin: Why the Emu Cannot Fly*. Magabala Books, 1993. Accessed 16 Dec 2017. https://web.archive.org/web/20070828205513//http://magabala.com/authors/authatoh2.htm#a4
Choo, Christine. *Mission Girls: Aboriginal Women on Catholic Missions in the Kimberley, Western Australia, 1900–1950*. University of Western Australia Press, 2001. Accessed 16 Dec 2017. https://www.findandconnect.gov.au/ref/wa/biogs/WE00023b.htm
McGregor, William B. "The Semantics, Pragmatics, and Evolution of Two Verbless Negative Constructions in Nyulnyul", *Oceanic Linguistics*, vol. 49, no. 1 (2010), pp.205–32. Accessed 16 Dec 2017. JSTOR, www.jstor.org/stable/pdf/40783591.pdf
Accessed 16 Dec 2017. http://www.hum.au.dk/ling/research/Kimberley%20languages%20map.htm
Accessed 16 Dec 2017. http://www.hum.au.dk/ling/research/Mary%20Carmel%20Charles.htm
Accessed 16 Dec 2017. http://www.hum.au.dk/ling/research/Nyulnyul%20facts.htm
Accessed 16 Dec 2017. https://www.findandconnect.gov.au/ref/wa/biogs/WE00023b.htm
Accessed 16 Dec 2017. https://www.australianstogether.org.au/discover/australian-history/stolen-generations

Theresa Hak Kyung Cha
Cha, Theresa Hak Kyung. *Dictée*. University of California Press, 1982. Epigraph.
De Sousa, Bea, and Desgorgues, Juliette. *A Portrait in Fragments: Theresa Hak Kyung Cha 1951–1982*. Whitmont Press, 2013. Accessed 11 Dec 2017. https://issuu.com/openshaw/docs/aportraitinfragments
Min, Pyong Gap. "Koreans' Immigration to the US: History and Contemporary Trends." New York:

The Research Center for Korean Community Queens College of CUNY, 2011. Accessed 11 Dec 2017. http://www.qc.cuny.edu/Academics/Centers/RCKC/Documents/Koreans%20Immigration%20to%20the%20US.pdf

Usow, Sophia. "The Fight Against Silence in Therese Hak Kyung Cha's *Dictée*", *Uncovered Classics*, 24 Mar 2016. Accessed 11 Dec 2017. http://www.uncoveredclassics.com/2016/03/24/the-fight-against-silence-in-theresa-hak-kyung-chas-dictee/

Wallach, Amei. "Theresa Cha: In Death, Lost And Found", *New York Times*, 20 Apr 2003. Accessed 11 Dec 2017. http://www.nytimes.com/2003/04/20/arts/art-architecture-theresa-cha-in-death-lost-and-found.html Accessed 11 Dec 2017. https://www.brookings.edu/articles/koreas-path-from-poverty-to-philanthropy/ Accessed 11 Dec 2017. http://www.peeruk.org/template-3/ Accessed 11 Dec 2017. http://www.robertatkins.net/beta/witness/artists/moves/tributes.html

Samira Azzam

Khalil-Habib, Nejmeh. "Al-Awda: the Theme of Return in Contemporary Arabic Literature: A Case-Study of Samira Azam", *Nebula* 5.5.2 (2008).

Khalil-Habib, Nejmeh. *Samira Azzam (1926–1967): Memory of the Lost Land.* Accessed 10 Dec 2017. http://www.nobleworld.biz/images/samiraazam.pdf

Piselli, Kathyanne. "Samira Azzam: Author's Works and Vision", *International Journal of Middle East Studies*, vol. 20, no. 1 (1988), pp.93–108.

Suleiman, Yasir. "Palestine and the Palestinians in the Short Stories of Samra 'Azzām", *Journal of Arabic Literature*, 1991, p.155. Accessed 10 Dec 2017. https://arablit.org/2017/08/17/must-read-classics-by-arab-women-writers-short-stories-by-samira-azzam/ Accessed 10 Dec 2017. http://www.bbc.co.uk/news/world-middle-east-39960461 Accessed 10 Dec 2017. http://www.jadaliyya.com/Details/30556/Samira-Azzam-A-Profile-from-the-Archives

Su Qing

Dooling, Amy. *Women's Literary Feminism in Twentieth-Century China.* Springer, 2005, p.158.

Huang, Nicole. *Women, War, Domesticity: Shanghai Literature and Popular Culture of the 1940s.* Brill Academic Publishers, 2005, p.4.

Ng, Janet. *The Experience of Modernity: Chinese Autobiography of the Early Twentieth Century.* University of Michigan Press, 2003.

Su Qing, "Waves", Silber, Cathy (trans.), Dooling, Amy D, and Torgeson, Kristina M (eds). *Writing Women in Modern China:*

An Anthology of Women's Literature from the Early Twentieth Century. Columbia University Press, 1998, pp.180–206. Accessed 21 Dec 2017. https://www.asymptotejournal.com/fiction/su-qing-ten-years-of-marriage/

Margaret Cavendish

Cunning, David, "Margaret Lucas Cavendish", *The Stanford.*

Holmes, Richard. "The Royal Society's Lost Women Scientists", *Guardian*, 21 Nov 2010. Accessed 6 Dec 2017. https://www.theguardian.com/science/2010/nov/21/royal-society-lost-women-scientists

Newcastle, Margaret Cavendish. *The Cavalier and his Lady: Selections from the Works of the First Duke and Duchess of Newcastle; edited with an introductory essay.* London Macmillan, 1872. Accessed 6 Dec 2017. https://archive.org/stream/cavalierandhisla00newcuoft/cavalierandhisla00newcuoft_djvu.txt

Sarasohn, Lisa T. *The Natural Philosophy of Margaret Cavendish: Reason and Fancy during the Scientific Revolution.* No. 2. JHU Press, 2010.

Zalta, Edward N (ed.). *Encyclopedia of Philosophy* (summer 2017), https://plato.stanford.edu/archives/sum2017/entries/margaret-cavendish

Zarelli, Natalie. "One of the Earliest Science Fiction Books Was Written in the 1600s by a Duchess", *Atlas Obscura*, 16 Sept 2016. Accessed 6 Dec 2017. https://www.atlasobscura.com/articles/one-of-the-earliest-science-fiction-books-was-written-in-the-1600s-by-a-duchess

Whitaker, Katie. "Duchess of scandal", *Guardian*, 8 Aug 2013. Accessed 6 Dec 2017. https://www.theguardian.com/world/2003/aug/08/gender.uk Accessed 6 Dec 2017. http://digital.library.upenn.edu/women/newcastle/blazing/blazing.html Accessed 6 Dec 2017. https://www.pepysdiary.com/diary/1667/04/11/ Accessed 6 Dec 2017. http://projectvox.org/cavendish-1623-1673/

Hermynia Zur Mühlen

Gossman, Lionel. *Liebe Genossin: Hermynia Zur Mühlen: A Writer of Courage and Conviction.* Accessed 3 Dec 2017. http://digital.library.upenn.edu/women/muhlen/gossman.html

Vietor-Engländer, Deborah. "Hermynia Zur Mühlen and the BBC" in Brinson, Charmian, and Dove, Richard (eds). *Stimme Der Wahrheit: German-language Broadcasting by the BBC.* Rodopi, 2003, pp 27–42.

Zur Mühlen, Hermynia. *The End and the Beginning: The Book of My Life.* Open Book Publishers, 2010. Accessed 2 Dec 2017. http://books.openedition.org/obp/433

Françoise de Graffigny

Bettam, Sean. "U of T researchers

ensure legacy of once-famous French author". Accessed 17 Dec 2017. http://news.artsci.utoronto.ca/all-news/completion-of-graffigny-project/

Bostic, Heidi. "Review". *Eighteenth-Century Studies*, vol. 42, no. 1, 2008, pp.175–177. JSTOR, www.jstor.org/stable/25161270

Bostic, Heidi. "The Light of Reason in Graffigny's Lettre d'une Péruvienne", *Dalhousie French Studies*, vol. 63, 2003, pp.3–11. JSTOR, www.jstor.org/stable/40837475

Bostic, Heidi. "Parisian and Peruvian Lives in Letters: Works by Françoise De Graffigny", *Eighteenth-Century Studies*, vol. 36, no. 4 (2003), pp.586–9. JSTOR, www.jstor.org/stable/30053612

Françoise de Graffigny, "Correspondance de Madame de Graffigny", tome 11: 2 juillet 1750–19 juin 1751, *Lettres 1570–1722*, Dainard, J A (gen. ed.); Arthur, Dorothy P (ed.); with Curtis, J; Ducretet-Powell, M-P; Showalter, English and Smith, D W. Voltaire Foundation, 2007.

Furbank, P N. "Jolly Bad Luck", *London Review of Books*, vol. 16, no. 6 (24 Mar 1994), pp.17–18. Accessed 17 Dec 2017. https://www.lrb.co.uk/v16/n06/pn-furbank/jolly-bad-luck

Showalter, English. "Graffigny at Cirey: A Fraud Exposed", *French Forum*, vol. 21, no. 1 (Jan 1996), pp.29–44. Accessed 17 Dec 2017. JSTOR, www.jstor.org/stable/pdf/40551915.pdf Accessed 17 Dec 2017. https://voltairefoundation.wordpress.com/2015/03/06/from-battered-wife-to-major-writer-madame-de-graffigny-and-her-tell-all-correspondance/

Neshani Andreas

Andreas, Neshani. *The Purple Violet of Oshaantu.* Heinemann Educational Books, 2001.

Fallon, Helen. "As Honest and Realistic as Possible: The Namibian Writer, Neshani Andreas", *Africa*, vol. 72, no. 2 (2007), pp.24–5. Accessed 6 Dec 2017. http://eprints.maynoothuniversity.ie/965/1/As_Honest_and_Realistic_as_Possible_Africa_March_2007_Vol_72_No_2.pdf

Wietersheim, Erika von. "Good-bye, Neshani! You did it your way: In remembrance of Neshani Andreas – Namibian author and passionate lover of words, a philosopher, a fighter for women's rights, an educator, a loyal Namibian, a friend", *Sister Namibia*, vol. 23, no. 2 (2011), pp.26+. Accessed 6 Dec 2017. https://www.namibian.com.na/index.php?id=79911&page=archive-read Accessed 6 Dec 2017. http://www.sahistory.org.za/article/namibian-struggle-independence-1966-1990-historical-background Accessed 6 Dec 2017. "Neshani Andreas: A Passion for Writing". The Free Library, 2004. *Sister Namibia.*

https://www.thefreelibrary.com/
Neshani+Andreas%3a+a+passion
+for+writing.-a0131994511

Radclyffe Hall
Popova, Maria. "November 9, 1928:
The Trial of Radclyffe Hall and
Virginia Woolf's Exquisite Case
for the Freedom of Speech",
Brainpickings. Accessed 26
November 2017. https://www.
brainpickings.org/2016/11/09/
well-of-loneliness-trial-of-radclyffe-
hall-virginia-woolf/
Souhami, Diana. *The Trials of
Radclyffe Hall*. Quercus, 2012, p.8.
Troubridge, Una. *The Life and Death
of Radclyffe Hall*. Hammond, 1961.
Accessed 6 Nov 2017. https://
ia600709.us.archive.org/9/items/
TheLifeAndDeathOfRadclyffe
Hallcorrected/0001.htm
Accessed 25 Nov 2017. "The Banned
Book", *Hull Daily Mail*, 16 Nov
1928. https://blog.britishnews-
paperarchive.co.uk/2013/11/15/
the-obscenity-trial-of-miss-radclyffe-
halls-novel-the-well-of-loneliness-
16-november-1928/

**HISTORIANS, ACADEMICS &
DIARISTS**
Esther Hillesum
Brandt, Ria van den. *Etty Hillesum:
An Introduction to Her Thought*. LIT
Verlag Münster, 2014.
Frenk, Hanan. "Etty Hillesum, 1914–
1943", *Jewish Women's Archive*.
Accessed 30 Dec 2017. https://jwa.
org/encyclopedia/
article/hillesum-etty
Hillesum, Etty. *Etty: The Letters
and Diaries of Etty Hillesum,
1941–1943*. Wm B Eerdmans
Publishing, 2002.
Woodhouse, Patrick. *Etty Hillesum:
A Life Transformed*. Bloomsbury
Publishing, 2009.

Anna Komnene
Kolovou, Ioulia. "Twelfth-century
Greek Byzantine Princess, Historian, Scholar – and Conspirator?"
Dangerous Women Project, 20 Apr
2016. Accessed 31 Dec 2017.
http://dangerouswomenproject.
org/2016/04/20/anna-komnene/
Komnene, Anna. *The Alexiad*. Franko-
pan, Peter (ed.) and Sewter, E R A
(trans.). Penguin Books Ltd, 2009.
Quandahl, Ellen, and Jarratt, Susan
C. "'To Recall Him…Will Be a
Subject of Lamentation': Anna
Comnena as Rhetorical Histori-
ographer", *Rhetorica: A Journal
of the History of Rhetoric*, vol. 26,
no. 3 (2008), pp 301–35. JSTOR,
www.jstor.org/stable/10.1525/
rh.2008.26.3.301
Neville, Leonora. *Anna Komnene:
The Life and Work of a Medieval
Historian*, Oxford University Press,
2016, p.166.
Newman, Barbara. "Byzantine
Laments", *London Review of
Books*, vol. 39, no. 5, 2 Mar 2017.
Accessed 31 Dec 2000. https://
www.lrb.co.uk/v39/n05/barbara-
newman/byzantine-laments

Marie Vassiltchikov
Annan, Gabriele. "Living Through the
War", 9 April 1987. Accessed 31 Dec
2017. http://www.nybooks.com/
articles/1987/04/09/living-through-
the-war/
Craig, Gordon A. "An Outsider
Inside the Third Reich", *New York
Times*, 5 April 1987. Accessed 31
Dec 2017. http://www.nytimes.
com/1987/04/05/books/an-
outsider-inside-the-third-reich.
html?pagewanted=all
Sheppard, R.Z. "The Catcher in
the Reich." *Time*, 24 June 2001.
Accessed 31 Dec 2017. http://
content.time.com/time/magazine/
article/0,9171,146374,00.html
Accessed 31 Dec 2017. http://www.
dialoginternational.com/dialog_
international/2016/07/review-the-
berlin-diaries-1940-1945-of-marie-
missie-vassiltchikov.html

Sei Shōnagon
Greer, David. "The Lists of a Lady-
in-Waiting", *Kyoto Journal*, no. 45.
Accessed 31 Dec 2017. http://
www.kyotojournal.org/the-journal/
culture-arts/the-lists-of-a-lady-in-
waiting/
McKinney, Meredith. "Meredith
Mckinney on Sei Shōnagon's
Masterpiece", *Kyoto Journal*, no.
67. Accessed 31 Dec 2017. http://
www.kyotojournal.org/the-journal/
in-translation/on-translating-a-
classic/
Mori, Kyoko. "Through the Bamboo
Blinds", *Fourth Genre: Explorations
in Nonfiction*, vol. 14, no. 1 (2012),
pp.147–58. JSTOR, www.jstor.org/
stable/41939162
Shikibu, Murasaki. *The Diary of
Lady Murasaki*. Bowring, Richard
(trans.). Penguin Classics, 1996.
Shōnagon, Sei. *The Pillow Book*. Mc-
Kinney, Meredith (trans.). Penguin
Books Ltd, 2005.

Carolina Maria de Jesus
Levine, Robert M. "The Cautionary
Tale of Carolina Maria de Jesus",
Latin American Research Review,
vol. 29, no. 1 (1994).
Maciel, Camille. "Brazil Remembers
Female Writer Who Defined Slums
as Trash Rooms in 1950s", *Agencia
Brasil*, 17 Mar 2013. Accessed 3
Jan 2017. http://agenciabrasil.ebc.
com.br/en/geral/noticia/2014-03/
brazil-remembers-female-writer-
who-defined-slums-trash-rooms-
1950s
Maria de Jesus, Carolina. *Child of the
Dark: The Diary of Carolina Maria
de Jesus*. Signet Classics, 2003.

Shen Shanbao
Fong, Grace S. *Herself an Author:
Gender, Agency, and Writing in
Late Imperial China*. University of
Hawaii Press, 2008.
Fong, Grace S. "Writing self and
writing lives: Shen Shanbao's
(1808–1862) Gendered Auto/
biographical Practices", *Nan Nü*,
vol. 2, no. 2 (2000).
Judge, Joan, and Hu, Ying (eds).
Beyond Exemplar Tales: Women's

Biography in Chinese History. Gaia
Books, 2011.
Lee, Lily Xiao Hong; Lau, Clara; and
Stefanowska, A D. *Biographical
Dictionary of Chinese Women: V.
1: The Qing Period, 1644–1911*.
Routledge, 17 Jul 2015.

Lili Elbe
Arken, *Gerda Wegener*.
Accessed 30 Dec 2017. https://
issuu.com/arken_museum/
docs/kataloguddrag_til_web_
uk/1?e=5419715/31841860
Beemyn, Genny. "Transgender
History in the United States" in
Erickson-Schroth, Laura (ed.).
Trans Bodies, Trans Selves. Oxford
University Press, 2014. Accessed
30 Dec 2017. https://www.umass.
edu/stonewall/sites/default/files/
Infoforandabout/transpeople/
genny_beemyn_transgender_
history_in_the_united_states.pdf
Caughie, Pamela L. "The Temporality
of Modernist Life Writing in the Era
of Transsexualism: Virginia Woolf's
Orlando and Einar Wegener's Man
into Woman", *MFS: Modern Fiction
Studies*, vol. 59, no. 3 (2013),
pp.501–25.
Elbe, Lili. *Man Into Woman: The First
Sex Change, a Portrait of Lili Elbe:
the True and Remarkable Transfor-
mation of the Painter Einar Wegener*.
Blue Boat Books, 2004.
Gailey, Nerissa, and Brown, A D.
"Beyond Either/Or: Reading Trans*
Lesbian Identities", *Journal of
Lesbian Studies*, vol. 20, no. 1
(2016), pp.65–86.
Meyer, Sabine. "Divine Interventions.
(Re)birth and Creation Narratives
in 'Fra Manð til kvinde-Lili Elbes
Bekendelser'", *Kvinder, Køn &
Forskning*, vol. 20, no. 2.
Minoff, Debra. "How True is 'The
Danish Girl'? Who are the real
Lili and Gerda?" *Screenprism*, 10
Jan 2016. Accessed 30 Dec 2017.
http://screenprism.com/insights/
article/the-danish-girl-how-much-
of-it-is-a-true-story

ESSAYISTS
Jane Anger
Anger, Jane. *Jane Anger her Protection
for Women. To defend them against
the scandalous reportes of a late
Surfeiting Lover, and all other like
Venerians that complaine to be
overcloyed with womens kindnesse*.
London: Richard Jones and Thomas
Orwin, 1589. Accessed 28 Nov
2017. http://digital.library.upenn.
edu/women/anger/protection/
protection.html
Ferguson, Moira (ed.). *First Feminists:
British Women Writers, 1578–1799*.
Indiana University Press, 1985.
Travitsky, Betty. "The Lady Doth Pro-
test: Protest in the Popular Writings
of Renaissance Englishwomen."
English Literary Renaissance, vol.
14, no. 3 (1984), pp.255–83.
Accessed 29 Nov 2017. JSTOR,
www.jstor.org/stable/
pdf/43447308.pdf
Accessed 29 Nov 2017. https://sites.

google.com/site/16thcenturybritish
literature/home/student-entries/
jane-anger Accessed 29 Nov 2017. http://
classics.mit.edu/Euripides/
andromache.html

Alice Dunbar-Nelson
Dunbar-Nelson, Alice Moore. "Brass
Ankles Speaks", unpublished.
Accessed 25 Nov 2017. http://
www.english.illinois.edu/maps/
poets/a_f/dunbar-nelson/essays.
htm
Dunbar-Nelson, Alice Moore. *Give
Us Each Day : The Diary of Alice
Dunbar-Nelson.* W W Norton, 1984.
Accessed 25 Nov 2017. https://
archive.org/details/giveuseachday
di00dunb
Hart, Betty. "A Cry in the Wilderness:
The Diary of Alice Dunbar-Nelson",
Women's Studies Quarterly, vol. 17,
no. 3/4, 1989, pp.74–8. JSTOR,
www.jstor.org/stable/40003094
Hull, Gloria T. *Give Us Each Day:
The Diary of Alice Dunbar-
Nelson.* Accessed 25 Nov 2017.
https://archive.org/stream/
giveuseachday00glor#page/20/
mode/2up/search/husband
Hull, Gloria T. "Researching Alice
Dunbar-Nelson: A Personal and
Literary Perspective", *Feminist
Studies,* vol. 6, no. 2, 1980,
pp.314–20. JSTOR, www.jstor.org/
stable/3177745.
Novak, Terry G. *Alice Dunbar
Nelson.* University of Minnesota, 2009. Accessed 25 Nov 2017.
https://conservancy.umn.edu/
bitstream/handle/11299/166289/
Nelson%2C%20Alice%20Dunbar.
pdf?sequence=1&isAllowed=y, p.2
Perry, Patsy B. "Signs", *Signs,* vol. 12,
no. 1, 1986, pp.174–6. JSTOR,
www.jstor.org/stable/3174369.

Marianna Florenzi-Waddington
Bacinetti Florenzi Waddington,
Marianna. "Pantheism as the
Foundation of the True and the
Good" in Copenhaver, Brian P, and
Copenhaver, Rebecca (eds). *From
Kant to Croce: Modern Philosophy
in Italy, 1800–1950.* University of
Toronto Press, 2012.
Commire, Anne, and Klezmer,
Deborah (eds). *Women in World
History: A Biographical Encyclopedia,*
vol. 2. Gale/Cengage Learning, 2002.
Kersey, Ethel M, and Schrag, Calvin O.
*Women Philosophers: A Bio-Critical
Source Book,* Greenwood Press, 1989.
Accessed 21 Dec 2017. http://
ludwigthefirst.weebly.com/
marianna-florenzi.html

May Ziade
Ghorayeb, Rose. "May Ziadeh
(1886–1941)", *Signs: Journal of
Women in Culture and Society,* vol.
5, no. 2 (1979).
Samman, Ghada, and Hassan, Fatme
Sharafeddine (ed.). "The Victim
Of Beauty: Reviving the Literary
Legacy of Mai Ziadeh", *Al Jadid,*
vol. 5, no. 28 (summer 1999).
Accessed 1 Dec 2017. http://www.
aljadid.com/content/victim-beauty-

reviving-literary-legacy-mai-ziadeh
Ziegler, Antje. "May Ziadeh
Rediscovered". Accessed 1 Dec
2017. http://web.archive.org/
web/20010114205100/http://leb.
net:80/~mira/isis/z/ziegler.html
Accessed 1 Dec 2017. https://
middleeastrevised.com/2014/
10/30/remembering-may-ziadeh-
ahead-of-her-time/
Accessed 1 Dec 2017. "Remembering May Ziadeh: Ahead of (her)
Time", *Middle East Revised,* 30 Oct
2014. https://middleeastrevised.
com/2014/10/30/remembering-
may-ziadeh-ahead-of-her-time/

Kāterina Te Heikōkō Mataira
Christchurch City Libraries. "Inter-
view with Kāterina Mataira", 2002.
Accessed 26 Nov 2017. http://
my.christchurchcitylibraries.com/
new-zealand-childrens-authors/
katerina-mataira/
Millar, Nadine. "Poet and Politician:
Sir Āpirana Ngata", *The Sapling,* 14
Sept 2017. Accessed 26 Nov 2017.
https://www.thesapling.co.nz/
single-post/2017/09/15/Poet-and-
Politician-Sir-%C4%80pirana-Ngata
Smith, Glenn. "Empowering
Language Revitalization", *Taiwan
Today,* 1 Feb 2015. Accessed 26 Nov
2017. http://taiwantoday.tw/news.
php?unit=12,29,33&post=23755
Smith, Kristen. "Te Atea: ko tenei te
wa: Kristin Smith", *The Sapling,* 11
Sep 2017. Accessed 26 Jan 2017.
https://www.thesapling.co.nz/
single-post/2017/09/15/Te-Atea-
ko-tenei-te-wa-Kristin-Smith
Storylines. "Dame Kāterina Te
Heikōkō Mataira", Storylines, no
date listed. Accessed 26 Nov 2017.
https://www.storylines.org.nz/
Storylines+Profiles/Profiles+I-M/
More+in+Profiles+I-M/Dame+
Katerina+Te+Heikoko+Mataira.
html
Turia, Tariana and Sharples, Pita.
"Passing of Dame Kāterina Te
Heikōkō Mataira", *Scoop Media,* 16
July 2011. Accessed 26 Nov 2017.
http://www.scoop.co.nz/stories/
PA1107/S00302/passing-of-dame-
katerina-te-heikoko-mataira.htm
Accessed 26 Nov 2017. https://
nzhistory.govt.nz/culture/maori-
language-week/history-of-the-
maori-language

Shulamith Hareven
Chomsky, Noam. *Fateful Triangle: The
United States, Israel, and the Pales-
tinians.* South End Press, 1999.
Farhi, Moris. "Shulamith Hareven:
Voice of the Levant", *Jewish
Quarterly,* vol. 38, no. 4 (1991).
Accessed 1 Dec 2017. http://www.
tandfonline.com/doi/abs/10.1080/
0449010X.1991.10705815
Joffe, Lawrence. "Shulamit Hareven",
Guardian, 13 Feb 2004. Accessed
1 Dec 2017. https://www.the
guardian.com/news/2004/feb/13/
guardianobituaries.booksobituaries
Hareven, Shulamith. "On Being a
Levantine", *PN Review,* Manchester,
vol. 18, no. 4 (1 Mar 1992).
Accessed 1 Dec 2017.

https://search.proquest.com/
openview/6772b4d6f022ce
60130dcbe32964feb5/1?pq-
origsite=gscholar&cbl=1817849
Hertzberg, Arthur. "100 Years Later,
a Jewish Writer's Time Has Come",
New York Times, 31 Mar 1991.
Accessed 1 Dec 2017. http://
www.nytimes.com/1991/03/31/
books/100-years-later-a-
jewish-writer-s-time-has-come.
html?pagewanted=all
Accessed 1 Dec 2017. http://www.
nytimes.com/1992/03/17/books/
writers-whose-fiction-stays-free-of-
politics.html?pagewanted=all
Accessed 2 Dec. https://jwa.org/
encyclopedia/article/hareven-
shulamith
Accessed 1 Dec 2017. https://jwa.
org/encyclopedia/article/hareven-
shulamith

Lucrezia Marinella
Allen, Prudence, and Salvatore,
Filippo. "Lucrezia Marinelli and
Woman's Identity in Late Italian
Renaissance", *Renaissance and
Reformation/Renaissance et
Réforme,* 17 (1992). Accessed 3
Dec 2017. JSTOR, www.jstor.org/
stable/43444859
Deslauriers, Marguerite, "Lucrezia
Marinella", *The Stanford Encyclo-
pedia of Philosophy* (Winter 2012
Edition), Edward N Zalta (ed.).
Accessed 3 Dec 2017. https://plato.
stanford.edu/archives/win2012/
entries/lucrezia-marinella
Frize, Monique. *Laura Bassi and
Science in 18th Century Europe:
The Extraordinary Life and Role of
Italy's Pioneering Female Profes-
sor.* Springer Science & Business
Media, 2013. Accessed 3 Dec 2017.
https://books.google.co.uk/books
?id=POa9BAAAQBAJ&q=lucrezia
+marinelli#v=snippet&q=lucrez
ia%20marinelli&f=false
Kolsky, Stephen. "Moderata Fonte,
Lucrezia Marinella, Giuseppe Passi:
An Early Seventeenth-Century
Feminist Controversy", *The
Modern Language Review* (2001),
pp.973–89. Accessed 3 Dec 2017.
https://www.jstor.org/stable/
pdf/3735864.pdf

JOURNALISTS & EDITORS
The Girl Stunt Reporters
Bly, Nellie. "Chapter XIV: Some
Unfortunate Stories", *Ten Days in
a Mad-House.* Ian L Munroe, 1887.
Accessed 6 Jan 2018. http://
digital.library.upenn.edu/women/
bly/madhouse/madhouse.html
Cartwright, R L. "Meet the Reporter
Who Blew The Lid Off Exploitation
of Women by Minnesota's Garment
Industry", *Minneapolis Post,* 20
Jan 2015. Accessed 6 Jan 2018.
https://www.minnpost.com/
mnopedia/2015/01/meet-reporter-
who-blew-lid-exploitation-women-
minnesotas-garment-industry
Gay, Eva. "The Toiling Women", *St.
Paul Globe,* 1 Apr 1888. Accessed
6 Jan 2018. http://dlib.nyu.edu/
undercover/i-toiling-women-eva-

gay-aka-eva-mcdonald-aka-eva-valesh-st-paul-globe
Linneman, William R. "Humorous Views of Yellow Journalism", *Studies in American Humor*, vol. 3, no. 1 (1976), pp.22–33. JSTOR, www.jstor.org/stable/42573097
Lutes, Jean Marie. "Into the Madhouse with Nellie Bly: Girl Stunt Reporting in Late Nineteenth-Century America", *American Quarterly*, vol. 54, no. 2 (2002), pp.217–53. JSTOR, www.jstor.org/stable/30041927
Todd, Kim. "These Women Reporters Went Undercover to Get the Most Important Scoops of Their Day", *Smithsonian Magazine*, Nov 2016. Accessed 6 Jan 2018. https://www.smithsonianmag.com/history/women-reporters-undercover-most-important-scoops-day-180960775/#HxYI15SftueDtjPe.99
Winchester, Beth. "What Nellie Bly Exposed at Blackwell's Asylum, and Why It's Still Important", *Medium*, 26 Apr 2016. https://medium.com/legendary-women/what-nellie-bly-exposed-at-blackwells-asylum-and-why-it-is-still-important-4591203b9dc7

Jessie Redmon Fauset
Ammons, Elizabeth. "New Literary History: Edith Wharton and Jessie Redmon Fauset", *College Literature*, vol. 14, no. 3 (1987).
Fauset, Jessie Redmon. *Plum Bun*. Frederick A Stokes, 1928.
Fauset, Jessie Redmon. *The Chinaberry Tree: A Novel of American Life & Selected Writings*. UPNE, 1931.
Griffin, Erica Lorraine. "The Living Is (Not) Easy: Inverting African American Dreams Deferred in the Literary Careers of Pauline Elizabeth Hopkins, Jessie Redmon Fauset, and Dorothy West, 1900–1995. Diss. The University of Georgia, 2002. Accessed 6 Jan 2018. https://getd.libs.uga.edu/pdfs/griffin_erica_l_200212_phd.pdf
Hughes, Langston. *"Big Sea": The Collected Works of Langston Hughes*. University of Missouri Press, 2001.
Jerkins, Morgan. "The Forgotten Work of Jessie Redmon Fauset", *New Yorker*, 18 Feb 2017. Accessed 6 Jan 2018. https://www.newyorker.com/books/page-turner/the-forgotten-work-of-jessie-redmon-fauset
Johnson, Abby Arthur. "Literary Midwife: Jessie Redmon Fauset and the Harlem Renaissance", *Phylon*, vol. 39, no. 2 (1978). JSTOR, www.jstor.org/stable/274509
Scutts, Joanna. "Absent Friends – Jessie Redmon Fauset", *Open Letters Monthly*, 1 Sept 2011. Accessed 6 Jan 2018. https://www.open lettersmonthly.com/oblivion/
Stoeckl, Sarah. *Salon, Page, World: Jessie Redmon Fauset, Mabel Dodge Luhan, Gertrude Stein, and the Borderlands of Culture*. Utah State University, 2007.

Marie Le Jars de Gournay
Dezon-Jones, Elyane. "Marie le Jars de Gournay (1565–1645)". Sartori, Eva Martin, and Zimmerman, Dorothy Wynne (eds). *French Women Writers: A Bio-bibliographical Source Book*. Greenwood Publishing Group, 1991.
Horowitz, Maryanne Cline (trans.). "Marie De Gournay, Editor of the *Essais* of Michel de Montaigne: A Case-Study in Mentor–Protegee Friendship", *The Sixteenth Century Journal*, vol. 17, no. 3 (1986). JSTOR, www.jstor.org/stable/2540321
Larsen, Anne R (trans.). "A Women's Republic of Letters: Anna Maria Van Schurman, Marie De Gournay, and Female Self-Representation in Relation to the Public Sphere", *Early Modern Women*, vol. 3 (2008). JSTOR, www.jstor.org/stable/23541520

Noni Jabavu
Jabavu, Noni. *Drawn in Colour: African Contrasts*. John Murray, 1960.
Makhosazana. "Noni Jabavu: A Peripatetic Writer Ahead of Her Times", *Tydskrif vir Letterkunde*, vol. 46, no. 1 (2009). Accessed 7 Jan 2018. http://www.scielo.org.za/scielo.php?script=sci_arttext&pid=S0041-476X2009000100017
Masola, Athambile. "Reading Noni Jabavu in 2017", *Mail & Guardian*, 11 Aug 2017. Accessed 7 Jan 2018. https://mg.co.za/article/2017-08-10-00-reading-noni-jabavu-in-2017
Mokoatsi, Thapelo, and Xaba, Phindile Xaba. "Pioneer: Helen Nontando (Noni) Jabavu (1919–2008)", *The Journalist*. Accessed 7 Jan 2018. http://www.the journalist.org.za/pioneers/pioneer-helen-nontando-noni-jabavu
Xaba, Makhosazana. "Noni Jabavu: A Peripatetic Writer Ahead of Her Times", *Tydskrif vir Letterkunde*, vol. 46, no. 1 (2009). Accessed 7 Jan 2018. http://www.scielo.org.za/scielo.php?script=sci_arttext&pid=S0041-476X2009000100017
Accessed 7 Jan 2018. "Call to Restore Noni Jabavu Legacy". *The Daily Despatch*, 31 Jan 2013. https://www.pressreader.com/south-africa/daily-dispatch/20130131/281883000718312

Dorothy Todd
Carrod, Amanda Juliet. "A Plea for a Renaissance": Dorothy Todd's Modernist Experiment in British Vogue, 1922–1926. Diss. Keele University, 2015, p.240.
McDowell, Colin. "100 Years of British Vogue", *Business of Fashion*, 4 Feb 2016. Accessed 5 Jan 2018. https://www.businessoffashion.com/articles/colins-column/100-years-of-british-vogue
Miralles, Nina-Sophia. "Vogue Legends: Two Editors & Their Lesbian Love", *LNDR* magazine, 22 July 2015. Accessed 5 Jan 2018.

http://www.londnr.com/fashion-art/vogue-legends-lesbian-vogue-editors/
Reed, Christopher. "Design for (Queer) Living: Sexual Identity, Performance, and Decor in British Vogue, 1922–1926", *GLQ: A Journal of Lesbian and Gay Studies*, vol. 12, no. 3 (2006): pp.377–403.
McDowell, Colin. "100 Years of British Vogue", *Business of Fashion*, 4 Feb 2016. Accessed 5 Jan 2018. https://www.businessoffashion.com/articles/colins-column/100-years-of-british-vogue
Miralles, Nina-Sophia. "Vogue Legends: Two Editors & Their Lesbian Love", *LNDR* magazine, 22 July 2015. Accessed 5 Jan 2018. http://www.londnr.com/fashion-art/vogue-legends-lesbian-vogue-editors/
Reed, Christopher. "Design for (Queer) Living: Sexual Identity, Performance, and Decor in British Vogue, 1922–1926", *GLQ: A Journal of Lesbian and Gay Studies*, vol. 12, no. 3 (2006): pp.377–403.

Marguerite Higgins
Bigart, Homer. *Forward Positions: The War Correspondence of Homer Bigart*. University of Arkansas Press, 1992.
Higgins, Marguerite. *News is a Singular Thing*. Doubleday, 1955.
Higgins, Marguerite. *War in Korea*. Doubleday & Co., 1951, p.17.
Keeshen, Kathleen Kearney. "Marguerite Higgins: Journalist, 1920–1966", Ph.D diss. University of Maryland, 1983
Knox, Donald, *The Korean War: Pusan to Chosin: An Oral History*. Harvest Books, 2002.
Murray, Peter Noel. "Marguerite Higgins: An Examination of Legacy and Gender Bias", Diss. University of Maryland, 2003. Accessed 1 Jan 2018. https://drum.lib.umd.edu/bitstream/handle/1903/47/dissertation.pd
Pride, Mike. "The Jury Has Spoken", *Columbia Journalism Review*, Spring 2016. Accessed 1 Jan 2018. https://www.cjr.org/the_feature/the_jury_has_spoken.php
Sofsky, Wolfgang. *The Order of Terror: The Concentration Camp*. Princeton University Press, 2013.
White, Stephen. "Letter to Richard Kluger", 15 Oct 1981, Box 16, Folder 348, Richard Kluger Papers. Manuscripts and Archives, Yale University Library.
Accessed 1 Jan 2018. "Marguerite Higgins hits 'Red Beach'", Pulitzer.org. http://www.pulitzer.org/article/marguerite-higgins-hits-red-beach

Allegra Lockstadt

Allegra Lockstadt was born in Canada, raised in the southeastern United States, and currently resides in Minneapolis, Minnesota, US. She currently works as freelance illustrator and designer. To see more of Allegra's work visit **www.allegralockstadt.com**

Sara Netherway

Lauren Simkin Berke

María Hergueta

Sara Netherway is an illustrator from the Isle of Wight. Originally trained in fine art, she enjoys creating images with rich textures and detail. To see more of Sara's work visit **www.saranetherway.co.uk**

Lauren Simkin Berke is an American artist and illustrator based in Brooklyn, NY. Working in ink on paper, Lauren draws for clients such as *The New York Times*, *Smithsonian* magazine, Simon & Schuster publishers and Rémy Martin. **www.simkinberke.com**

María Hergueta is a freelance illustrator from a small village in north Spain. She has been working as an illustrator for five years now and her work has been published in different publishing houses and magazines such as Oxford University Press, Penguin Books and *The New York Times*.

She currently lives between Barcelona and the Swedish countryside.

Miriam Castillo

Miriam Castillo is an illustrator based in Brooklyn and Mexico. Her whimsical hand-drawn illustrations explore the intersection in between yoga, spirituality and nature. For more of her world, visit **www.miriamcastillo.com**

Marcela Quiroz

Marcela works as an illustrator for publishing projects and print media. Her day is divided between books and pencils, searching for new words, memorizing them and writing them over and over again until they become drawings and part of some of her alphabets of illustrated words.

www.do-re-mi.co

Shreyas R Krishnan

Shreyas is an illustrator-designer from Chennai, India. She is curious about the ways in which art, design and gender intersect. Through drawing and writing, she tries to understand how, why and what we remember.

www.shreyasrkrishnan.com

Grace Helmer

Grace Helmer is a
Brighton-born, London-
based illustrator.
She has put her
paintbrushes to work
for a range of clients,
including Apple,
Google, HarvardX and
Marie Claire.

www.gracehelmer.co.uk

Tanya Heidrich

Tanya is a Swiss,
American and German
graphic designer and
illustrator who designs
in colour and illustrates
in black and white
drawing inspiration
from patterns and
details in everyday life.

www.tanyaheidri.ch

W T Frick

Winnie T Frick is
a comic artist and
illustrator currently
based in Brooklyn.
Her interests include,
cross-hatching,
architecture and
doppelgängers.
Her illustrations
and webcomics can
be found on
www.ipsumlorum.com

Hélène Baum

Hélène Baum is a
Berlin-based illustrator.
"There are no lines
in nature, only areas
of colour, one against
another" (Manet). This
principle guides her
work and life. With
her diverse cultural
background and
much travelling, she
creates a cosmic space
through which humour,
idealism and elements
from diferent cultures
co-exist in vibrant
images.

The New Historia

In creating this series, the author and publisher have worked with Gina Luria Walker, Professor of Women's Studies at The New School, New York City, and Director of The New Historia, carefully building, curating and editing the list of 48 women within this book to ensure that we uncovered as many lost female histories as possible. The New Historia's ongoing work is dedicated to the discovery, recovery and authoritative reclamation of women of the past through time and around the globe, and honour earlier women by telling their stories and sharing their strategies that inspire us to be sturdy and brave. In them we find our foremothers, transforming and remaking our ideas about history and ourselves.

"It is imperative that we galvanize what we know so that women's legacy is acknowledged as essential to the continuum of human enlightenment. Activating what we know will also keep us from making contemporary women invisible – waiting to be brought to life 50 or 100 years from now."
Gina Luria Walker,
The New Historia

www.thenewhistoria.com

I would like to thank the first person who ever encouraged me as a reader and writer: my mother. Thank you for enrolling me in creative writing classes, buying me books, and never once rolling your eyes when I wanted to visit another bookshop or library.

Thank you to everyone at Octopus, including but most especially Romilly Morgan and Pauline Bache. To all the Women Who Draw illustrators, whose work never fails to stun me. To Dr Gina Luria Walker at the New Historia, for her insight and help. To my agent at Rogers, Coleridge & White, Emma Paterson, and my constant support, Daniel Johnson. To Kate Lloyd, Natasha Wynarcyzk, David Woode, and all my other old friends and fellow journalists from City. Never stop writing.

Zing Tsjeng

The Publisher would like to thank the entire team involved in curating the list of women featured in *Forgotten Women: The Writers*, and in particular would like to praise The New Historia centre's ongoing work in rediscovering women's contributions throughout history.